KOMINKA

*The Beauty and Wisdom of
Japanese Traditional Folk Houses*

KAZUO HASEGAWA

MUSEYON
NEW YORK

© 2024 Kazuo Hasegawa

All rights reserved. No part of this publication may be copied or transmitted in any form by any means, electronic, mechanical, recording or otherwise, except brief extracts for the purpose of review, and no part of this publication may be sold or hired without the express permission of the publisher.

Library of Congress Cataloging-in-Publication Data

Names: Hasegawa, Kazuo, 1946- author. | Alex Child, translator.
Title: Kominka : the beauty and wisdom of Japanese traditional folk houses / Kazuo Hasegawa.
Other titles: Kominka saisei monogatari. English
Description: New York : Museyon, [2024] | Includes index.
Identifiers: LCCN 2024002004 (print) | LCCN 2024002005 (ebook) | ISBN 9781940842707 (hardcover) | ISBN 9781940842714 (ebook)
Subjects: LCSH: Architecture, Domestic--Japan. | Wooden-frame houses--Japan. | Vernacular architecture--Japan. | BISAC: ARCHITECTURE / Historic Preservation / General
Classification: LCC NA7451 .H2713 2024 (print) | LCC NA7451 (ebook) | DDC 728/.370952--dc23/eng/20240301
LC record available at https://lccn.loc.gov/2024002004
LC ebook record available at https://lccn.loc.gov/2024002005

Published in the United States and Canada by:
Museyon Inc.
2322 30th Rd.
LIC, NY 11102

Museyon is a registered trademark.
Visit us online at www.museyon.com

ISBN 978-1-940842-70-7 (Print)
ISBN 978-1-940842-71-4 (eBook)

Printed in China

For Hajime, Rei, and Chie

CONTENTS

INTRODUCTION *8*

I REDISCOVERING OLD JAPAN'S KOMINKA

What Is a Kominka? *12*

Foreigners Captivated by the Charms of Kominka *19*

Alex Kerr and Chiiori *20*

Shelley Clarke and Kawasemi Cottage *26*

II 101 UNFORGETTABLE KOMINKA EXPERIENCES

Kominka Maps *37*

My Top Tier (1–32) *50*

More Great Choices (33–101) *188*

III MY KOMINKA ODYSSEY AND DIARY

1980s–2007—The Journey Begins *242*

2008–2009—Finding Perfection *246*

2010—Rebuilding the Kominka *260*

2011—Finishing the Job *300*

VENUE INFORMATION *383*

ACKNOWLEDGMENTS *401*

INDEX *402*

INTRODUCTION

Why am I so obsessed with Japan's traditional old houses, known as kominka?

My career as the publisher of a housing magazine, *Jutaku Joho*, during Japan's postwar industrial and economic boom has a lot to do with it. Starting around 1980, I traveled the length and breadth of Japan for my publication, reviewing the newest, latest, most advanced housing that modern construction technology could provide. High-rise condominiums, single-family dwellings, custom-built houses, residential developments in major urban centers, including the Tokyo metropolitan area: I included them all in the pages of my publication—and in my life. Born in Kyoto in the year following the end of World War II, I moved with the times, changing residence sixteen times by last count. Each newly built residence promised me a comfortable lifestyle. Yet the only thing I felt was discomfort.

New Japanese houses lacked character. Worse, as I traveled the country for my job, I saw that quality kominka in rural communities and historic towns were either being demolished or abandoned, in the name of progress. I asked myself if this was right. The answer was no, of course. I documented the destruction and decay with photographs, releasing them to the public in newspaper and magazine articles or in solo exhibitions. Additionally, my extensive travels abroad to more than eighty countries confirmed that beautiful old houses existed all over the world, were lovingly restored, and consequently were reborn. Why was this not happening in Japan? Soon, the beauty and culture of traditional folk houses became the overriding theme of my life and work. Something had to be done to preserve Japan's past before it was too late. So, in 1997, I helped establish the Japan Minka Revival Association (JMRA) to protect and preserve traditional Japanese houses. And I made a solemn promise to myself: One day, I would live in a kominka of my own.

Part I of this book examines the cultural significance of kominka. It also proves the universal appeal of kominka by introducing you to two Americans who have immersed themselves in the traditional Japanese way of life. Part II is essentially a guide to my favorite kominka and historic villages; it is meant to inspire exploration and discovery, whether you are a first-time visitor to Japan or a return traveler.

The more I saw and experienced of Old Japan, the more I wanted to protect and preserve a piece of it for myself, my family, and future generations. After many twists and turns, my dream came true. My diary in Part III, originally published in 2022 in Japan as a stand-alone, how-to book, *Kominka Saisei Monogatari*, chronicles my journey to find and restore the traditional kominka I now call home.

I

REDISCOVERING OLD JAPAN'S KOMINKA

WHAT IS A KOMINKA?

A kominka is an old house, but not just any old house. A kominka is a "traditional" Japanese old house.

Constructed according to time-honored timber frame methods, kominka houses are scattered throughout Japan. They are found along the coast, in the mountains, and in remote rural hamlets, once powerful castle towns, hospitable post towns, and spiritual temple towns. They range from fishing village folk cottages and thatched-roof farmhouses to merchant mansions and dwellings for lower-ranked samurai. And since each region in Japan has its own unique culture and climate, a region's old houses reflect and accommodate those conditions.

As to how old a building made of wood must be before it can be classed as a kominka, that is open to debate. The Japanese government's Agency for Cultural Affairs opts for a minimum of fifty years. But, it can be argued that it is more appropriate to set the age at a hundred years or more. In the decades following the end of World War II in 1945, Japan entered a period of accelerated industrialization and modernization. With the nation on a fast track, cost-effective and time-saving construction shortcuts took

What Is a Kominka?   13

precedence in the booming economy over the painstakingly skillful and aesthetically pleasing methods of bygone eras.

The history of wooden architecture in Japan owes much to the nation's rich forests which produce an abundance of high-quality timber. Since ancient times, sturdy pillars, exposed beams, and rafters—not walls—have defined the structural framework of a traditional Japanese timber frame house. This classic type of architecture, where the pieces fit together as in an intricate puzzle without the help of nails, screws, glue, and power tools, employs techniques unchanged for generations and requires a high level of carpentry expertise.

By contrast, framework wall architecture—introduced from the West at the end of the Edo period (1603–1867) and the beginning of the Meiji era (1868–1912) and often referred to as the conventional construction method in postwar Japan—advocates box-like structures supported by walls and floors made of framed lumber and structural plywood. Partition walls made in a factory and precut lumber are assembled at the construction site using braces, nails, and attached metal hardware. Concrete and molded

The structural framework of a traditional Japanese timber frame house

plastic are other "modern" building materials that have taken the place of solid wood.

Today, the overwhelming majority of wooden frame houses in Japan are built using conventional construction methods, while only about one percent or so are built using traditional timber frame construction methods. "Cookie-cutter" houses are quick and cheap to build, but they have no soul. Nor are they built to last. The life expectancy of a new wooden frame house in Japan has been estimated at around thirty years—sometimes more, but often less—due to poor construction as much as wear and tear. Compare this to a traditional kominka, which can be as old as several hundred years and still escape the devastating damage brought about by the heavy snowfalls, tycoons, tsunamis, and earthquakes to which Japan is vulnerable.

More and more people in reaction against postwar uniformity, the prefab culture, and the deleterious effect modernization and Westernization have had on Japan's architecture, village communities, and natural landscapes now look to our nation's rich history to regain a significant part of the cultural heritage they believe we have lost.

Foremost among the reactionaries was Tsunekazu Nishioka (1908–1995), one of Japan's most revered master carpenters and a passionate, often outspoken champion of the traditional timber frame construction method. Born into a family of temple and shrine carpenters who had practiced their craft for four centuries, Nishioka was heir to techniques that had been handed down since the Asuka period (592–710). For example, it was he who revived the use of ancient carpentry tools such as the yari-ganna (spear plane). But two high-profile projects in Nara Prefecture in the 1970s and early 1980s truly defined his career and reputation as a master builder: the reconstruction of the Kondo (Main Hall) and the West Pagoda of the Yakushiji Temple, and the dismantling and repair of the world's oldest existing wooden structure—the Buddhist Horyuji Temple complex dating from the year 607.

The five-story pagoda at Horyuji Temple

Nishioka's participation in these restorations was not without controversy, however. He clashed loudly and publicly with academicians who insisted that Western repair methods—reinforced steel frames, bolts, and concrete—supplement traditional restoration methods. Japanese universities at that time boasted departments specializing in Western architecture but none that were dedicated to the study and research of traditional Japanese wooden architecture. Moreover, the government was on the side of the universities. It seemed like an uphill battle, but Nishioka dug in his heels. Japanese scholars of Western architecture were theorists with no practical experience, he argued. Craftsmen build while scholars merely observe, he argued further. Nishioka stood his ground, and, in the end, he won out, rebuilding the temples using traditional methods and with only a few modern compromises.

The firestorm of controversy brought on by newspaper and TV coverage of these events ignited an interest in traditional Japanese architecture and traditional construction methods. So, too, did Nishioka's own books, which proved that he was as articulate with words as he was adept with his hands. Consequently, wooden architecture slowly began to gain favor in the universities and in the public imagination.

It goes without saying that not all wooden architecture in Japan is as grand or as imposing the Horyuji complex. Humbler examples abound in the form of kominka houses. In 1997, the Japan Minka Revival Association (JMRA), a nonprofit organization and grassroots movement, was formed. JMRA, which continues and thrives today, is most definitely not a passive agent of nostalgia. Rather, it actively endorses and pursues the maintenance, preservation, and revitalization of kominka houses as a vital way to restore a sense of identity to the Japanese people and to recapture the simple joys of the traditional Japanese lifestyle. This is not to say that rejuvenating a kominka precludes updating kitchen and bath facilities, two mainstays of modern-day life. On the contrary, the goal is to establish a harmonious balance between both worlds—traditional and contemporary, past and present.

Woodworking skills

From left, thatched roofing, a joint, a kumiko wood panel

Moreover, as kominka houses are refurbished, they are repurposed not just as private homes for well-to-do families. They also become shops, galleries, museums, inns, bed and breakfasts, coffeehouses, teahouses, and restaurants for everyone to experience and enjoy.

The United Nations Educational, Scientific, and Cultural Organization (UNESCO) has also contributed to the growing interest in Japan's wooden architecture. Having already designated the historic monuments and temples in Nara as UNESCO World Heritage Sites, the organization in 2020 evaluated Japan's traditional skills and techniques for the conservation and transmission of wooden architecture and decided to register them on its Representative List of the Intangible Cultural Heritage of Humanity. The seventeen skills include woodworking; plastering; tile, bark, shingle, and thatched roofings; and the making of tatami mats for flooring. Techniques used in the decoration, coloring, and lacquering of building exteriors and interiors are also registered. Since many of these skills were instrumental in creating kominka houses and are now employed in restoring the buildings, registering them helps ensure that there will be craftspeople with the ability—and the will—to preserve kominka now and in the future.

The renewed interest in this aspect of Japan's past also recognizes the low impact a kominka has on the environment. Since a kominka's building materials—wood, soil, paper, straw, and stone—come from nature, this is the ultimate sustainable architecture. Nor can the importance of kominka to the Japanese tourist industry be underestimated. For many travelers, international as well as local, visiting and/or staying at a kominka is more than a step back into Old Japan. It is a step forward into the real Japan.

As I travel around my native country, I cannot help but appreciate the wonder of our traditional old houses while photographing them. What do I see through my viewfinder?

Thatched roofs that gracefully curve; thick, shiny black pillars that rise majestically as in a cathedral; translucent shoji screens that diffuse light. Mortise and tenon joints are as beautiful—and photogenic—as a work of sculpture, while the intricate geometric patterns of cedar and cypress kumiko decorations have meanings and tell stories that go beyond mere ornamentation. As I focus my lens, I see beauty and simplicity. But I also feel. I feel at home.

It never ceases to amaze me that the charms of kominka are not the work of a single master carpenter or a famous architect, but are instead the work of many unknown carpenters and workmen whose lived experience in every Japanese region informs their ingenuity, skill, and craft. No two kominka are alike, and so I find myself in a state of perfect rapture every time I press the shutter.

FOREIGNERS CAPTIVATED BY THE CHARMS OF KOMINKA

On my travels around Japan I meet many fascinating people who, like me, have been seduced by the irresistible attraction of kominka. Moreover, you don't have to be Japanese to fall in love with kominka. Two Americans—Alex Kerr and Shelley Clarke—stand out for their unwavering commitment and enthusiastic dedication to the traditional Japanese way of life. These successful professionals could live anywhere in the world, yet they have chosen to set down roots in Japan. Why? As you will discover in the interviews that follow, their reasons for doing so are varied and profound. I hope that you will have the opportunity to visit and experience their remarkable kominka properties, just as I did. In giving new life to old houses, these pioneers from over the seas are true friends of Japan.

ALEX KERR AND CHIIORI

Alex Kerr, an American-born Japan lover for nearly sixty years, is a man of many talents: a scholar of Oriental culture, with degrees in Japanese Studies from Yale University and Chinese Studies from Oxford University; a calligrapher; a collector of East Asian art and antiques; an architecture and landscape critic; and a journalist. His published books in which he offers an appreciative—if often critical—perspective on Japanese culture, traditions, and public works are widely read throughout the world and include *Lost Japan* (1993 Japanese, 1996 English), *Dogs and Demons: The Fall of Modern Japan* (2001 English, 2002 Japanese), and *Living in Japan* (2006 English). And, like me, Kerr is a big fan of kominka, having rescued and refurbished traditional folk houses all over Japan.

I visited Hanare Ninoumi, a kominka inn in Kameoka, Kyoto Prefecture, restored by Kerr, to find out how he became interested in old Japanese houses. I also sought out his thoughts on how best to preserve Japan's natural landscapes and traditional beauty before they disappear.

HASEGAWA: When you were twelve, your father, a United States Navy officer, was posted to Japan. What was that like for you?

KERR: It was a dreamlike experience, now that I think about it. At that time there were wonderful mansions in Tokyo and Yokohama, where we lived, and I visited them with my mother. Japanese houses fascinated me. The Western-style houses I had known until then had a living room as soon as you entered the front door and, in some cases, you could see the stairs leading to the upper floor. But with the layout of a Japanese house you don't see everything all at once. There's an entrance foyer, an earthen floor, a wooden hallway, and a middle room. Also, by opening the sliders, or removing the fittings, you can catch a glimpse of the back of the house. It felt mysterious, and I liked that. I still do.

HASEGAWA: Did anything else impress you at that time?

KERR: The mountains and coast of Japan. I also liked temples. Later on, in 1971 during my summer vacation from Yale, I traveled all around Japan, from Hokkaido to Kyushu. At the end of the trip, my Japanese friend took me to the Iya Valley on his motorcycle. "You will love it here," he said.

HASEGAWA: Twenty years ago, I went to Ochiai Village in Iya. To get there, you have to go deep into the mountains on a narrow road between two steep valleys along the Iya River. Even then, few Japanese people went there, and it is amazing that you were able to go there in 1971. Did you love it as your friend said you would?

KERR: I did. In Europe, there are many villages on top of mountains. However, in the traditional Japanese rural landscape, shrines and temples typically sit atop a mountain, while people live at the foot of the mountain and rice paddies spread out around them. But Iya is quite different. People actually live on the slopes of the mountains. The land is carved out; the terrain is steep; and thatched houses are scattered around the cliffs. There are no dense settlements. It was truly mysterious in its unparalleled appearance, as if it had come out of a Chinese hanging scroll.

From left, Alex Kerr and Kazuo Hasegawa

古民家 ♦ *Kominka*

Top and above, Chiiori; *left,* Iya Valley

CHIIORI
篪庵(ちいおり)
Kominka Inn
*209 Tsurui, Higashi-Iya,
Miyoshi, Tokushima*

HASEGAWA: Did you ever think that you would buy a house in Iya?

KERR: On a subsequent trip to Iya a few years later, I noticed that there were many abandoned and vacant houses, and I thought, "Oh, maybe I could buy one." So, I started looking. I walked through many Iya hamlets before finally arriving at the thatched farmhouse I eventually purchased. "This is my castle!" I said in my heart. I was confident that if I fixed it up, it would be not only livable, but splendid. I named it "Chiiori"—"House of the Flute"—because I play the flute.

HASEGAWA: When did you decide to make Japan your home?

KERR: After graduation from Oxford, I returned to Japan and the Oomoto seminary in Kameoka, where I worked and learned a great deal about traditional Japanese culture—the tea ceremony, Noh, kobudo [classical martial arts], and calligraphy. I didn't have a house to live in, so I looked for a vacant house in Kameoka and found an old house in the grounds of Yada Tenmangu Shrine. I still live there. I am not sure how many hundreds of years ago the house was built, but it was moved once in the Edo period, around the middle of the 18th century, so it must be at least 300 years old. When I first saw it, it looked like a haunted house. It was covered with cobwebs, and the tatami floor was rotting. When I tried to open the storm door on the porch, the whole thing fell apart because of the rotting boards. But it was that moment that made me decide to rent the house. Beyond the shutters was a view of the moss-covered backyard and the woods and stream beyond. I was struck by what a wonderful house it was. I call it my never-ending and eternal kominka project.

HASEGAWA: Your experience in Iya led you to the "Kyoto Project," which you started in 2004. I was born in Kyoto and know all about the many restrictions Kyoto places upon real estate development. How difficult was it for you?

KERR: When I came to convert machiya houses [traditional wooden townhouses] in Kyoto into modern and comfortable lodging facilities for foreigners and locals alike, I was faced with Kyoto's Fire Protection Law, the Building Standard Law, laws related to cultural properties, laws related to lodging, and various other laws and regulations from different governing authorities. Most people, I think, would be discouraged when confronted with these laws and regulations. They would say, "Forget it, let's just replace the old house with a new, comfortable house instead of preserving the old one." I understand that feeling. But I held on, thinking, "You can't give up here!"

HASEGAWA: What kept you going?

KERR: Anger. Every time I went abroad and came back, I saw the destruction of the Japanese cityscapes and landscapes that I loved so much. I felt nothing but despair when I saw the above-ground electric wires, telephone poles, billboards, concrete, and plastic sheeting that covered Japan. While Japanese people were thinking, "We are the number one economic power in Asia," other Asian countries were making much more advanced efforts and moving ahead of Japan in terms of tourism and environmental awareness. My mentor, Masako Shirasu, a connoisseur of Japanese beauty, was a strict and scary teacher. One day, she said to me, "If you love someone, you must be angry with them." I think she was right. But anger must be turned into something positive. In this case, the revitalization of Japanese culture, including kominka.

HASEGAWA: What kominka villages would you recommend to foreign visitors?

KERR: First of all, Kameoka. There are many beautiful kominka along the road from Kameoka to the Sea of Japan via Sonobe, Ayabe, and Fukuchiyama. Next, Iya. I am very happy that Iya has been established as a hidden treasure of the travel industry. I have also seen many wonderful villages in the Tohoku region.

Hanare Ninoumi

HASEGAWA: And what about the future?

KERR: It is very important to preserve and inherit the precious landscapes, townscapes, architecture, and culture that are unique to Japan because of the serious challenges posed by globalization. We need to think about economic growth as an extension of sustainability. One model for this is efforts to revitalize traditional folk houses and the various initiatives surrounding them. I continue to travel all over the world. Perhaps it is my nature not to settle down in one place, yet I will always be deeply rooted in Japan.

HANARE NINOUMI
離れ にのうみ
Kominka Inn
15 Nishitatsu, Kameoka, Kyoto

SHELLEY CLARKE AND KAWASEMI COTTAGE

Fascinated by Japan's rich nature, traditional culture, and old houses, American Shelley Clarke has settled in Sasama, a remote and depopulated mountain village in Shizuoka Prefecture. Born and raised in a fishing village in Maine, Clarke holds an undergraduate degree in Zoology from the University of North Carolina–Chapel Hill, a master's degree in Fisheries and Marine Policy from the University of Washington, and a PhD in Quantitative Fisheries Science from Imperial College London. After seeing a photo of the scientist dressed in a kimono, sitting on the floor and playing the koto (Japanese harp), I knew I had to meet and interview her about her passion for the kominka lifestyle. My late wife also was a koto player.

Taking the Tokaido Shinkansen (bullet train) from Tokyo, I transferred to the Oigawa Railway, a local line, at Kanaya Station. The Oigawa Railway is famous for its steam locomotives running along the Oigawa River. It took forty minutes to reach Kawane Onsen Sasamado Station. From the station, the car ran through beautiful tea plantations and along mountain roads for twenty minutes. Finally, we arrived at Shelley Clarke's wonderful old house.

HASEGAWA: How did you become interested in Japan?

CLARKE: When I was twenty-one and a student, I spent two months as an inspector aboard a Nippon Suisan vessel which was fishing for Alaska pollock in the Bering Strait and other areas of the Bering Sea. Nippon Suisan's vessels were fishing within 200 nautical miles of the United States and, as a condition of their permit, I was required to monitor their catch. All of the crew members except me were Japanese, and I became interested in Japanese culture through socializing with them. They were very polite and well mannered. I also learned about Japanese food in the cafeteria and Japanese culture through the TV news.

HASEGAWA: When did you come to live and work in Japan?

CLARKE: After completing my doctorate, I was accepted to a Japanese government scholarship program and came to Japan in 2003. The scholarship period was for eleven months, and the theme was fisheries research. I lived in Shimizu in Shizuoka Prefecture and worked with Japanese shark researchers.

Shelley Clarke

HASEGAWA: Did you live in a kominka?

CLARKE: I lived in Numazu next door to Shimizu, but not in a kominka. Still, I was very excited to be there, enjoying the baths, tatami rooms, and shoji screens that are characteristic of Japanese private houses. The longer I lived there, my desire to stay in Japan grew stronger, and I began to think that I wanted to live in a farmhouse with an old Japanese atmosphere in order to better understand the Japanese way of life. So I began looking for a farmhouse around Shimizu. I visited the mountain village of Sasama on a cycling trip and was attracted by the beautiful satoyama landscape. Then, in 2005, a real estate agent I knew helped me find and buy my first traditional folk house, and I moved there.

HASEGAWA: You must have liked the countryside to choose to live so deep in the mountains.

CLARKE: I grew up in a small town in rural Maine, so living in a mountain village was no problem for me. When I first saw the farmhouse, I didn't know anything about it, but it made a

古民家 ♦ *Kominka*

A sunken hearth

wonderful impression. Western-style houses hide wood, but the farmhouse had thick wood that really stood out. I liked its pillars and its hearth, which I rebuilt. While living in the farmhouse, I found the property where we are sitting now on a walk and was curious about it. It seems that the house was originally the residence of the village head, a former timber merchant. When the elderly homeowner passed away, the house became vacant and his sons, who live elsewhere, abandoned it. I thought it was a waste to see weeds growing in the garden. About three years after finding it, I asked a neighbor, "Would they sell this house if someone wanted to buy it?" He said, "They may." He was surprised because I raised my hand right then and there. I thought it was fate.

HASEGAWA: The estate is large and has several buildings . . .

CLARKE: There are ten buildings on the property. They include the main house, where I live; a detached cottage, which I have renovated into a guesthouse; a teahouse, which I remodeled and opened as a cafe in 2020; two fireproof storehouses, one of which

Kawasemi Cottage

is now a public bathhouse; a storage room for tableware and food; a silkworm loft; an oinari-san [a small shrine] built in the Meiji era; and two barns. The main house was built over a hundred years ago and was extensively remodeled in the 1950s. Other buildings, like the oinari-san, are older.

HASEGAWA: How did you go about settling in?

CLARKE: First, I cleared out the trash from the houses and repaired the damaged oinari-san. The original owners were not close to their neighbors because of their powerful position as head of the village. So I wanted to create a new connection with the locals by rebuilding the oinari shrine. I now make offerings of water, sake, salt, and rice at the shrine on the first day of every month. I also wanted to welcome the locals into the house, so I built a sunken hearth and had drinking parties.

HASEGAWA: What was your biggest concern when you decided to convert the detached cottage into an inn for paying guests?

Top, Sasama offers beautiful walks in nature; *bottom,* Shelley Clarke dedicates a kagura dance

CLARKE: I asked a local carpenter to help me preserve the traditional architectural style. We have kept the retro charm of the old days, while also respecting the need for modern-day comforts. You can see the river from here. I sometimes see kawasemi [kingfishers] early in the morning, so I named the inn Kawasemi Cottage.

HASEGAWA: What building did you work on next?

CLARKE: The old teahouse, but it was severely damaged and difficult to renovate. The theme of the renovation is nostalgia for the Showa era of the 1960s. I decorated with furniture and furnishings that had been kept in the storehouse, as well as retro home appliances purchased online. I wanted to give the cafe a name that would pair with Kawasemi Cottage, so I chose Hotaru [Firefly], partly because fireflies come to the bank of the pond. Our signature dishes are espresso and homemade muffins. Local people help run the cafe.

HASEGAWA: On my way here, I asked directions to the "American woman's house." Everyone knows you, Shelley, and I was told to visit your cafe. The coffee, they told me, is delicious! But all this—the house, the land, and the renovations—must have cost you quite a bit.

Chaya Hotaru

CLARKE: Yes. And the renovations are not finished yet, so it will cost even more. But that is not an issue. This is an investment in the charms of Sasama.

HASEGAWA: Enjoying kominka living at Kawasemi Cottage is probably the first priority for a visitor, but what other fun things does this area offer?

CLARKE: Shizuoka Prefecture is known for its mild climate, beautiful forests, and well-kept tea plantations. There are several trails, offering small walks to full-blown hikes. I recommend that visitors take a walk in nature, get in the water or sit on a rock and soak their feet while enjoying the flow of the river. Cycling here is great. The roads are steep and strenuous, but if you are prepared for that, this is a cyclist's paradise. However, you will need a road bike or mountain bike. There is also a hot spring twenty minutes away by car. Horseback riding, grass skiing, paragliding, and other out-of-the-ordinary pleasures are also available. In Sasama, there is the 300-year-old tradition of kagura, a dance dedicated to the gods, which I have taken up. Finally, the Oigawa Railway, one of the few regular steam locomotive lines in Japan, makes one or two round trips per day, attracting many railroad fans.

HASEGAWA: What would you like to achieve in the future?

CLARKE: Sasama is my home. I am very happy to live here and give back to the people of Sasama. However, with the aging and depopulation of the area, in about twenty years I may be the only one left. I want to avoid that and find people who want to live here. To that end, I want to introduce the charms of Sasama to as many tourists as possible. I hope that people—Japanese and foreigners—who fall in love with Sasama will decide, as I did, to live here.

KAWASEMI COTTAGE AND CHAYA HOTARU
カワセミ コテージ・茶屋 蛍
Kominka Inn and Cafe
1323 Kawane Sasamakami, Shimada, Shizuoka

II
101 UNFORGETTABLE KOMINKA EXPERIENCES

Compiling a list of Japan's most charming kominka and villages for a traveler from overseas to experience was, at first, easy. I immediately thought of more than 200. But then came the hard part. I had to whittle the list down to a more manageable 101 for this book. I use the word "whittle" on purpose. As I trimmed, carved, and planed the list, I likened myself to a carpenter in the Edo period making a kominka by whittling pine, cedar, and cypress trees into pillars, beams, sliding doors, and latticed windows.

Every list of recommendations is, by its very nature, subjective. And mine is no exception. Only authentically old houses and traditional villages that I have visited, eaten at, stayed at—and loved—made the final cut. If I have allowed a few modern (less than 100 years old) structures to sneak in, I did so to point out the role traditional values play both now and in the future. Another condition for inclusion: The buildings and facilities on the final list had to still be in use. Also, I have shied away from the famous to focus on the lesser known. It is possible I have omitted worthy kominka and villages. But that is why I travel. While I have visited traditional homes and villages in Japan for over forty years, there are many, many more for me to discover. And that excites me.

Some foreigners may think of Japan as a small island nation. However, Japan's territory stretches approximately 1,900 miles from northern Hokkaido, a cold region, to the southern Okinawa and Pacific islands with their subtropical climate. Japan is blessed with diverse natural beauty and rich cultural heritage. In each climate and terrain, needless to say, there are traditional homes and villages that reflect local character and identity. With this list as a guide, the ultimate choice of where to go is yours to make. But if I have one request, it is this: No matter how you reach your destination, whether by airplane, train, bus or rental car, once you are there I ask (I could say, insist) that you walk around. There is no better way to interact with local people and experience Old Japan. The truth is, once you have arrived, the journey has only just begun.

KOMINKA MAPS

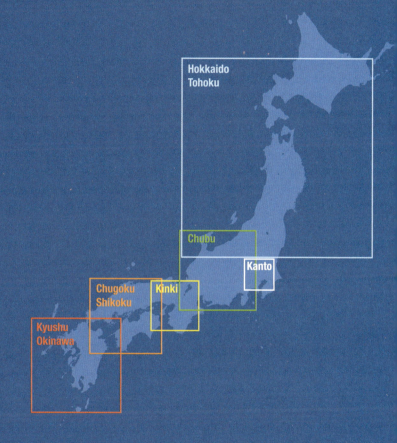

Hokkaido Tohoku

		Kanji Characters
1	Esashi Town	江差
2	Kaitaku no Mura	開拓の村
3	Kakunodate	角館
4	Ginzan Onsen	銀山温泉
5	Ouchijuku	大内宿
8	Sado Island	佐渡島
33	Hakodate Motomachi	函館元町
34	Otaru Canal	小樽運河
35	Kuroyu Onsen Inn	黒湯温泉
36	Tateiwa Village	舘岩村
37	Kitakata	喜多方

Japan Basin

Index

- Bullet Train
- Railroad
- National Highway
- Hot Spring

Yamato Rise

Sado Island

Sado Island 8

Joetsu Shinkansen

Toyama Bay

Ishikawa   Hokuriku Shinkansen

2500ft
100km

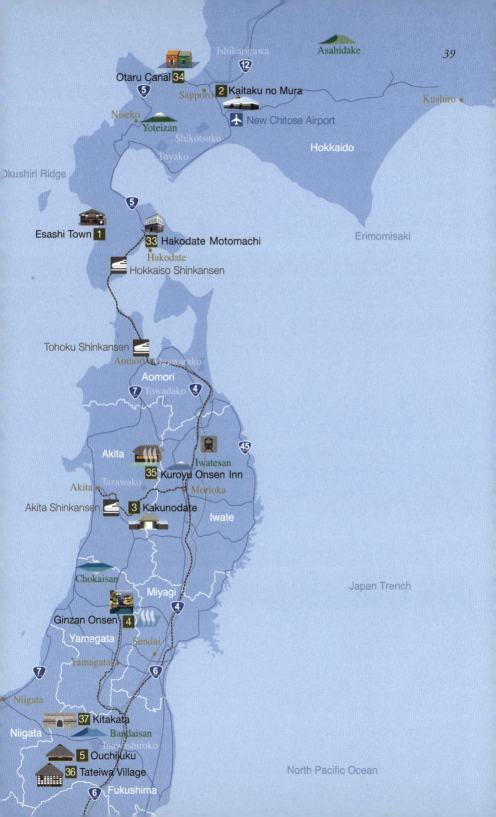

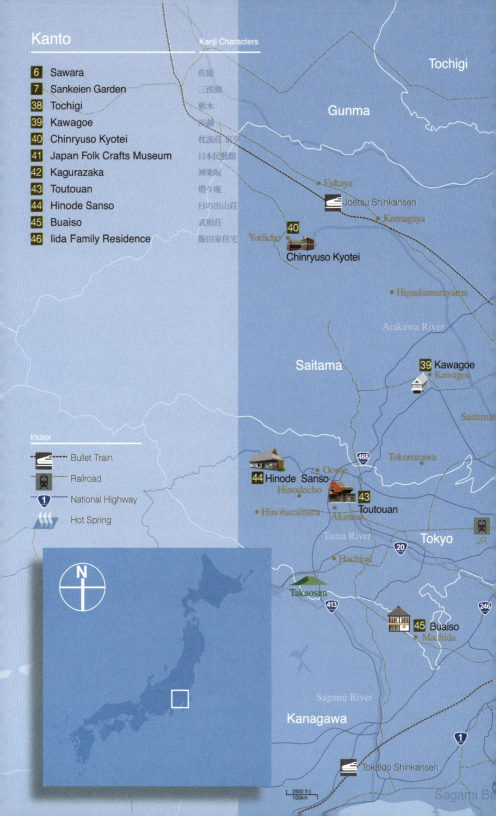

Chubu

		Kanji Characters
C	Kawasemi Cottage & Chaya Hotaru	カワセミ コテージ・茶屋 蛍
D	Kazui Family Residence	敷井家住宅
E	Hideaway	ハイダウェイ
9	Matsudai Bengs House	松代ベンクスハウス
10	Unnojuku	海野宿
11	Sangoso & Minamigaoka Art Museum	三五荘・南ヶ丘美術館
12	Matsumoto	松本
13	Tsumago	妻籠
14	Yamanashi Kominka Club	山梨古民家倶楽部
15	Shirakawago & Gokayama	白川郷・五箇山
16	Hida Takayama & Hida Furukawa	飛騨高山・飛騨古川
17	Sekijuku	関宿
47	Oginoshima Village	荻ノ島
48	Sankyoson	散居村
49	Kanazawa	金沢
52	Oshino Village	忍野村
53	Aoni	青鬼
54	Obuse	小布施
55	Naraijuku	奈良井宿
56	Koshinzuka	こうしんづか
57	Mugeiso	無藝荘
58	Kasenan Seni Onsen Iwanoyu	花仙庵 仙仁温泉 岩の湯
59	Gero Onsen Yunoshimakan	下呂温泉 湯之島館
60	Mino	美濃
61	Numazu Club	沼津倶楽部
62	Izu Matsuzaki	伊豆 松崎
63	Kakujoro	角上楼

		Kanji Characters
64	Arimatsu	有松
65	Asuke	足助
66	Shiratama	志ら玉
97	Katakurakan	片倉館

Index

- Bullet Train
- Railroad
- National Highway
- Hot Spring

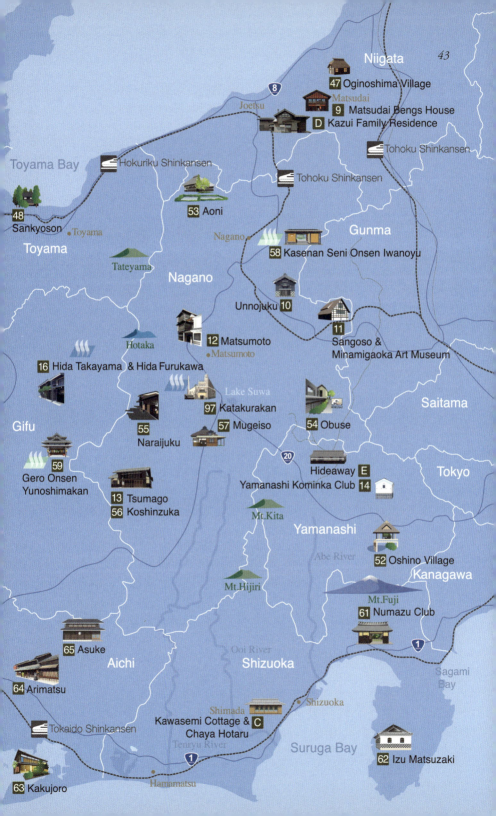

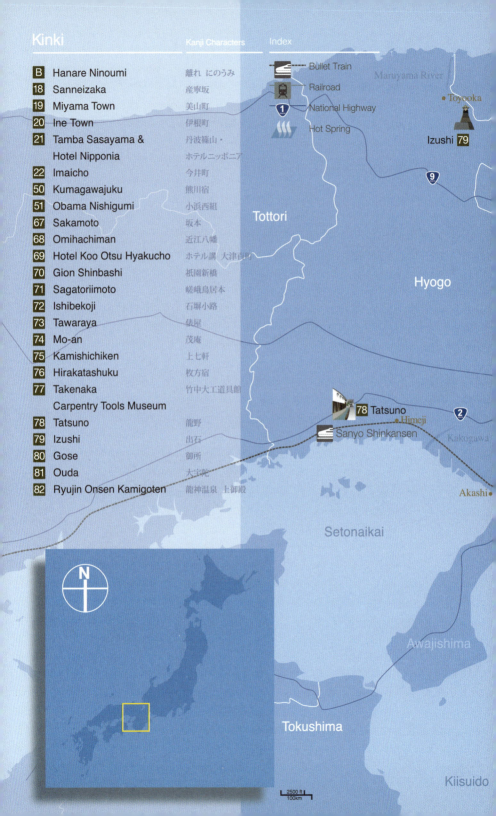

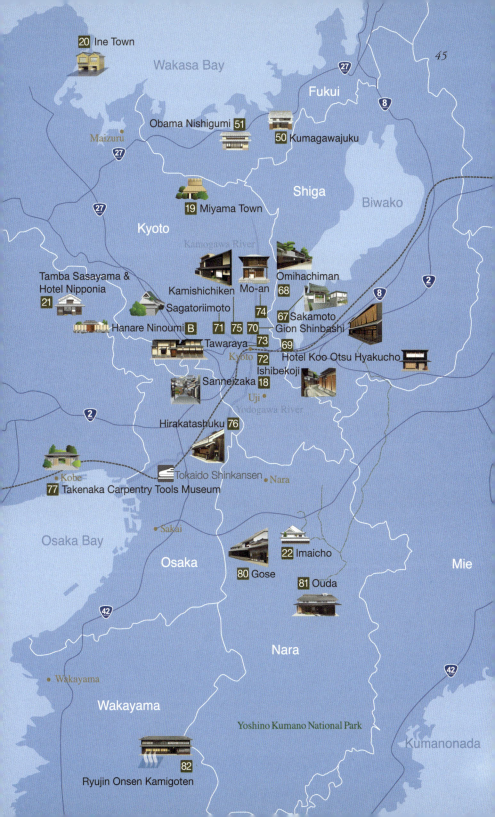

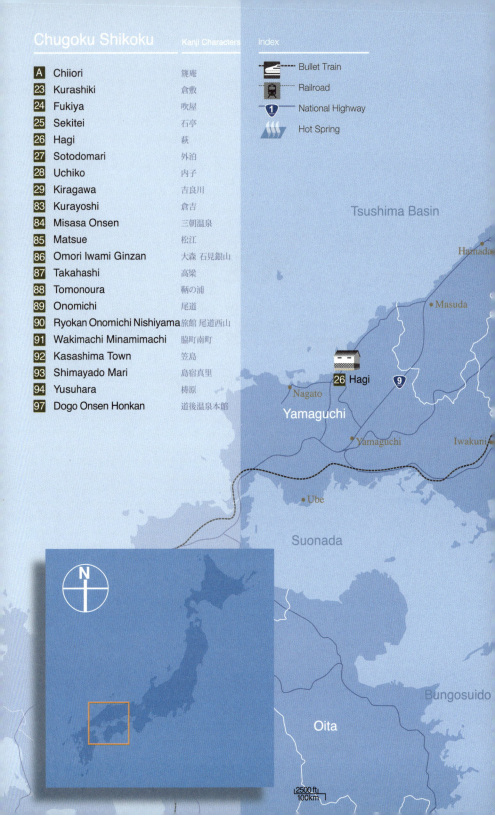

Kyushu Okinawa

		Kanji Characters
30	Kitsuki	杵築
31	Sanso Murata	山荘 無量塔
32	Taketomi Island	竹富島
95	Yanagawa	柳川
96	Tachibana-tei Ohana Estate	立花邸 御花
97	Takegawara Onsen	竹瓦温泉
98	Usuki	臼杵
99	Gajoen	雅叙苑
100	Izumifumoto	出水麓
101	Chiran	知覧

Sasebo
Nagasaki
Nagasaki

Index

- Bullet Train
- Railroad
- National Highway
- Hot Spring

East China Sea

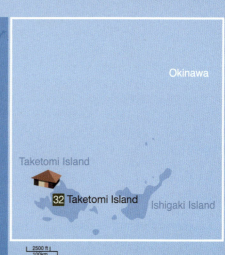

Okinawa
Taketomi Island
32 Taketomi Island
Ishigaki Island

2500 ft / 100km

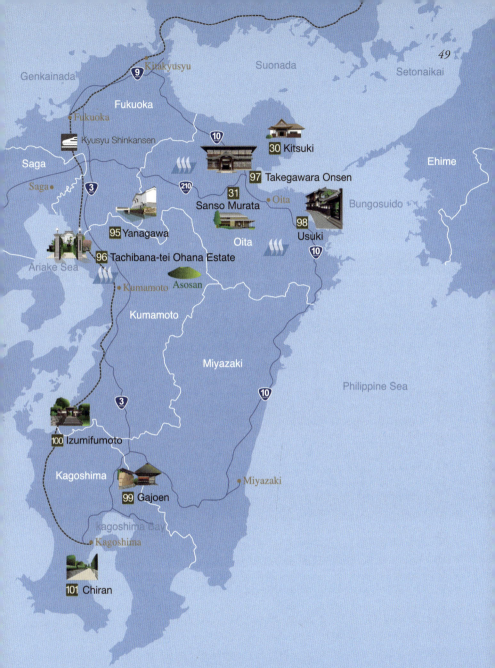

MY TOP TIER

- ❶ Esashi Town 江差
- ❷ Kaitaku no Mura 開拓の村
- ❸ Kakunodate 角館
- ❹ Ginzan Onsen 銀山温泉
- ❺ Ouchijuku 大内宿
- ❻ Sawara 佐原
- ❼ Sankeien Garden 三溪園
- ❽ Sado Island 佐渡島
- ❾ Matsudai Bengs House 松代ベンクスハウス
- ❿ Unnojuku 海野宿
- ⓫ Sangoso & Minamigaoka Art Museum 三五荘・南ヶ丘美術館
- ⓬ Matsumoto 松本
- ⓭ Tsumago 妻籠
- ⓮ Yamanashi Kominka Club 山梨古民家倶楽部
- ⓯ Shirakawago & Gokayama 白川郷・五箇山
- ⓰ Hida Takayama & Hida Furukawa 飛騨高山・飛騨古川
- ⓱ Sekijuku 関宿

- ⑱ Sanneizaka 産寧坂
- ⑲ Miyama Town 美山町
- ⑳ Ine Town 伊根町
- ㉑ Tamba Sasayama & Hotel Nipponia 丹波篠山・ホテル ニッポニア
- ㉒ Imaicho 今井町
- ㉓ Kurashiki 倉敷
- ㉔ Fukiya 吹屋
- ㉕ Sekitei 石亭
- ㉖ Hagi 萩
- ㉗ Sotodomari 外泊
- ㉘ Uchiko 内子
- ㉙ Kiragawa 吉良川
- ㉚ Kitsuki 杵築
- ㉛ Sansou Murata 山荘無量塔
- ㉜ Taketomi Island 竹富島

① ESASHI TOWN
江差
Hokkaido

Above left, Nakamura Family Merchant House

Luxurious Palaces in Northern Japan

Esashi—a natural harbor town facing the Sea of Japan on Hokkaido, the northernmost of Japan's four main islands—was inhabited by the indigenous Ainu people before it became a Japanese territory in the 16th century. The town flourished in the early 18th century as a center of the herring fish industry.

古民家 ◆ *Kominka*

Clockwise from top: The Yokoyama merchant family has lived in the same house since 1822; a replica of the Japanese frigate *Kaiyomaru*; a traditional warehouse

Many grand private houses in Esashi survive from this period of wealth, including the Nakamura Family Merchant House (a National Important Cultural Property) and the Sekikawa Family Villa (a Hokkaido Tangible Cultural Property). Collectively, they are known as the "Herring Palaces" for the obvious reason: Their owners made their fortunes from fishing for herring. In addition to these "palaces," the town has many other traditional-style houses, either with the entrance under a gabled roof or built as storehouses. Esashi may be small, but its townscape is the most spectacular in Hokkaido.

In 1868, during the Meiji Restoration—when imperial rule under the emperor replaced the feudal/military form of government under the samurai—the Tokugawa shogunate's army, after being defeated in battle, fled to Esashi aboard the *Kaiyomaru*, a state-of-the-art wooden ship built in the Netherlands. As it neared Esashi, the *Kaiyomaru* encountered a storm, ran aground, and sank. Today, a replica of the *Kaiyomaru* is a tourist attraction on Esashi's wharf; the ship's original cannons and portions of the hull were salvaged from the sea and are on display.

Thanks to various activities throughout the year that tell the story of Esashi's history, culture, and traditions, the town has been recognized by Japan's Agency for Cultural Affairs as a Japan Heritage site.

ESASHI TOWN
Historic Town
Esashi, Hokkaido

2 KAITAKU NO MURA
開拓の村
Sapporo, Hokkaido

The restored Aoyama family house (1919)–a herring palace–and its interior

Kominka Buildings That "Breathe"

People from different parts of Japan settled in Hokkaido from the Meiji period (1868) to the late Taisho (1912–1926) and early Showa (1920s) periods. As those immigrants put down roots in Hokkaido, they constructed buildings whose styles reflected the various regions from which they came. In order to preserve

58　古民家 ♦ *Kominka*

A 1911 police box relocated to Kaitaku no Mura from Minami Ichijo, Sapporo

the essence of this diverse cultural and architectural history, fifty buildings from all over Hokkaido were relocated to a forest on the outskirts of Sapporo, the principal city of the prefecture. The purpose-built community of Kaitaku no Mura opened in 1983 and includes a town, a fishing village, a farming village, and a mountain village.

Every building in the outdoor complex—from stately Western-style buildings to private homes, a noodle shop, a sake brewery, a Shinto shrine, a dairy barn, and even a police box—has been carefully restored. The entire facility is well managed and maintained in a spacious site with a natural environment that complements the traditional structures.

I have photographed many old and reconstructed kominka and villages, but I have never had much interest in or desire to photograph old buildings that are reconstructed and preserved as museums. I am only attracted to buildings which "breathe," as if people actually live and work there. To use an analogy, it would be

Kurumasa Inn (1919)

like a wildlife photographer taking pictures of taxidermied animals in a diorama instead of living animals in their natural habitats. That said, Kaitaku no Mura is well worth a visit for its creativity, ingenuity, and historical accuracy.

In Inuyama City, Aichi Prefecture, there is a similar and excellent facility called Museum Meiji-Mura, where about sixty epoch-making buildings built in the Meiji era have been relocated and restored.

KAITAKU NO MURA HISTORICAL VILLAGE OF HOKKAIDO
Museum
50-1 Atsubetsu, Sapporo, Hokkaido

③ KAKUNODATE
角館
Akita

The residence of the Aoyagi samurai family

The "Little Kyoto" of Akita

The castle town of Kakunodate, located in the center of Akita Prefecture on the island of Honshu, was founded in 1620 and ruled by a samurai descended from a noble family in Kyoto. Because of the town's geographical similarity to Kyoto, Kyoto culture was introduced in Kakunodate. Many place names are in the Kyoto style; and, on the bank of the Hinokinai River that runs west of the town, a two-kilometer-long tunnel of beautiful weeping cheery trees transported from Kyoto profusely flower every spring.

When the castle town was built, roads were widened, sewers were dug, and, as a fire prevention measure, vegetation was cleared to make way for a firebreak with an earthen mound in its center. The firebreak protected the town, but it also divided it by class and social standing. The part of the town to the north of the firebreak was Uchimachi (Inner Town), the residential area of the samurai; the part to the south was Tomachi (Outer Town), the residential area of tradesmen, craftsmen, and ordinary townsfolk.

In Uchimachi, the samurai quarter, there are deep groves of trees and stately mansions, such as the homes of the Aoyagi, Iwahashi, Ishiguro, and Matsumoto families which are open to the public. The national government has officially recognized Uchimachi, whose original state is well preserved and maintained, as an Important Preservation District for Groups of Traditional Buildings.

Merchant houses and businesses line Kakunodate's Outer Town. One of these, the Ando Miso Brewery—a family-owned brick warehouse and factory built in the early Meiji period (1868–1912)—deserves a visit; the brewery's artisanal miso and soy sauce can be tasted on the premises and purchased in the shop as delicious souvenirs of your visit.

A must-visit throughout the year, Kakunodate is particularly enchanting in spring when rows of ornamental Someiyoshino cherry trees turn walkways along the Hinokinai River into lush and fragrant promenades.

KAKUNODATE
Historic Castle Town
Kakunodate-machi, Senboku, Akita

Clockwise from top: Mansions line the streets of Uchimachi, Kakunodate's samurai district; shoji screens in a samurai residence; weeping cherry trees in bloom

◆ GINZAN ONSEN
銀山温泉
Obanazawa, Yamagata

An Ethereal Hot Spring Resort

This remote area in Yamagata Prefecture rose to prominence during the Muromachi period (1336–1573) when rich deposits of silver ore were discovered in 1456. The Nobesawa Ginzan silver mine, which prospered until the middle of the 17th century, closed in 1689, its lode nearly exhausted. But that's when

66   古民家 ◆ *Kominka*

Clockwise from top: Notoya Ryokan, built during the Taisho period (1912–1926); a "Taisho Roman" window at Notoya Ryokan is a Japanese interpretation of a Western arched window; enjoying a foot bath on one of Ginzan Onsen's promenades

GINZAN ONSEN
Historic Hot Spring
Obanazawa, Yamagata

Ginzan (the Japanese word for "silver mine") began its second life as a popular onsen (hot spring resort), whose thermal waters are said to have been unearthed by miners while digging for the precious metal. As fate would have it, a flood in 1925 destroyed the hot springs and many of the ryokan (traditional Japanese inns) that housed the spa's guests. Undeterred, the local business community reconstructed the area, creating today's romantic vacation destination, with its rows of multistory wooden inns built in the late-Taisho (1912–1926) and early Showa (1926–1989) periods along both banks of the Ginzan River. Pedestrian bridges cross the river, and the cobblestoned sidewalks are illumined by picturesque gas lamps, which, together with the lights of the ryokan, create an ethereal world from dusk to dawn. Foot baths and traditional public bathhouses along the promenades help soothe and relax travelers. In 1983, the charms of the onsen became nationally and internationally known when it was used as a setting for the hit Japanese TV drama *Oshin*.

Many of Ginzan's ryokan are grand three- and four-story traditional wooden structures, with exteriors decorated with trowel paintings. Notoya Ryokan is the most eye-catching. The building, on-site hot spring, food, and hospitality are all excellent; if you can book lodging here, your stay in Ginzan Onsen will be that much richer.

Since this is a snowy area, winter is one of the most photogenic times of the year to visit when the pristine white landscape has much to offer. If warm-weather events and entertainments are more to your liking, traditional Hanagasa Odori dance performances are held on Ginzan's bridges every weekend from May to October.

◆5 OUCHIJUKU
大内宿
Shimogo, Fukushima

A Traditional Post Town in the Edo Period

A post town is a stop on a highway that offers rest, food, and lodging to travelers. Ouchijuku, a traditional post town, was established in the middle of the 17th century (Edo period) on the Aizu Nishi Kaido mountain road, which connected Aizu-Wakamatsu, a castle town in the Fukushima Prefecture, with Nikko

古民家 ♦ Kominka

From top: Kominka soba-noodle restaurant, Misawaya; thatched hip roof kominka houses; Ouchijuku in winter

OUCHIJUKU
Historic Post Town
Shimogo-machi, Minami Aizu, Fukushima

and Imaichi in the Tochigi Prefecture. Ouchijuku prospered for approximately 200 years, with many of its inns reserved exclusively for government officials en route to and from Edo, the then-capital city. Eventually, in 1884 (early Meiji period), the town fell into decline when a new national highway opened and bypassed it. But that turned out to be a good thing: Ouchijuku is noteworthy today because it still retains the unspoiled vestiges of an Edo-period post town, with over thirty thatched hip roof kominka lined up along both sides of the old highway. Most of them were constructed between the late-Edo period and the Meiji period, and have ditches dug in front that provide them with flowing water.

Temples and shrines are integrated into this pleasing historical landscape. If you climb the stone steps of the shrine located on the hill at the back of the town, you will get a bird's-eye view of the structural and symmetrical beauty of the village from the top of the steps.

Ouchijuku—selected as an Important Preservation District for Groups of Traditional Buildings—has become very popular in recent years, and during the daytime, especially on weekends, it is crowded. If possible, spend the night at a guesthouse in the village, take a walk in the quiet of the evening after the tourists have left or in the early morning before they arrive, and immerse yourself in Ouchijuku's charming and authentic Edo atmosphere.

Koinobori (carp streamers) decorate Ouchijuku on Children's Day in May

6 SAWARA
佐原
Katori, Chiba

Sawara's nostalgic stores are still alive and active; *right*, the Sawara Grand Festival

A Retro River Town

The merchant town of Sawara began its long and prosperous history as a commercial and transportation center along the Tone River in the Edo period (1603–1867). The Tone, one of the longest rivers in Japan, flows from north to east through the Kanto region before emptying into the Pacific Ocean. It plays an

古民家 ♦ *Kominka*

Merchant houses with massive tile-roofed storehouses line the Ono River

important role in Japan's economy as a source of water for the Tokyo metropolis. The Ono River, a tributary of the Tone, serves as a canal in Sawara. Along its banks are many kominka, as well as dashi––stone steps used for loading boats in the old days. The atmospheric canal, townhouses, and steps are often used for movie locations. Merchant houses, built in storehouse style with massive tiled roofs and earthen walls covered with black plaster, dot the Katori Kaido highway, which crosses Sawara. Many buildings date from the late-Edo and Meiji periods, including the Shobundo bookstore, which has been around since the Edo period; Koboriya, a soba noodle shop; and Nakamuraya dry goods store.

More than 220 years ago, a native of Sawara, Ino Tadataka (1745–1818), retired from running his family's sake brewing business and handed over the reins of the business to his children. He took a new wife; and from the age of fifty-five, he spent seventeen years traveling on foot, making the first map of Japan.

The Sawara Grand Festival, a 300-year-old tradition, is held twice a year, in summer and fall

Today, the surveyor and cartographer is a role model for middle-aged and elderly people. His former residence in Sawara is a national historic site; his survey maps and surveying instruments are on display in the Ino Tadataka Memorial Hall, which lies across the Ono from his former residence.

Shobundo bookstore

SAWARA
Historic Merchant Town
Katori, Chiba

❼ SANKEIEN GARDEN
三溪園
Yokohama, Kanagawa

Rinshunkaku, the centerpiece of Sankeien's inner garden

A Businessman's Cultural Legacy

Sankeien Garden, created by Hara Sankei (1868–1939), a businessman who made his fortune in the silk trade, is located in the southeastern part of Yokohama, a metropolis overlooking Tokyo Bay. Within the vast garden's more than forty-three acres are seventeen buildings, including historically important temples,

Left to right: Rinshunkaku; this gassho-style residence was moved from Shirakawago, Gifu

pagodas, teahouses, and private houses that were moved here from Kyoto, Kamakura, and other cities. Architectural styles represented include the refined and elegant sukiya style and the more rustic gassho style characterized by a thick, steep, and slanting thatched roof that resembles two hands with their fingertips touching in prayer. Fun fact: A gassho-style roof is a godsend in winter since snow easily slides to the ground, helping to keep the thatch dry, exposed to sunlight, and therefore free of rot.

In addition to being an entrepreneur, Hara Sankei was one of Japan's foremost tea masters and art collectors, and while possessing many national treasures, he also nurtured and supported budding visual artists. Works by some of the leading modern Japanese painters, such as Yokoyama Taikan (1868–1958), are in the garden's fabled art collection. Many artists left their works behind after being invited to stay at the garden and paint it.

But Sankei was not motivated by self-interest. Nor did he create the garden solely for the pleasure of rich people. He was deeply concerned about the disappearance of the Japanese wa (harmony) culture and spirit due to the rapid Westernization of Japan after the Meiji Restoration in 1868 (coincidentally the year of his birth). He believed that culture belongs to everyone and is not the property of one privileged person or class. With this in mind, he opened the garden to the public in 1906. Several of the garden's traditional buildings host exhibitions, workshops, and civic events; it is also a popular venue to rent for weddings. As Hara Sankei would want, there is nothing stuffy or elitist about Sankeien Garden.

SANKEIEN GARDEN
*Kominka Houses and Garden
58-1 Honmokusannotani,
Naka-ku, Yokohama, Kanagawa*

❽ SADO ISLAND
佐渡島
Sado, Niigata

Clockwise from left: Sankakuya (the Triangular House) in Shukunegi; a car ferry connects Niigata and Sado Island in two and a half hours; Takigi Noh at Ushio Shrine

Japan's "Golden" Island

Sado Island in the Sea of Japan was once called home by many noblemen and literati who were banished from the capital of Kyoto around the 13th century. Today, the influence of the Kyoto-style culture these exiles brought with them can still be felt in the remote island's architecture, temples, and entertainments. For example, Sado's over thirty Noh stages account for almost half of the total number of Noh stages in Japan today. Sado is especially known for its Takigi (bonfire) Noh performances which take place on outdoor stages at night and are dramatically lit by crackling bonfires; shows are held almost every weekend from the end of April to October in various locations on the island.

During the 17th century, Sado was one of the world's leading producers of gold—some say the world's largest producer of pure gold at that time. Gold is no longer mined on the island, but remnants from that era include the mining town of Aikawa, whose kominka-lined main street, Kyomachidori (Kyoto Town Street), pays tribute to Kyoto with sections named Shimokyo, Nakagyo, and Kamikyo, among others. Every June, scores of dancers in traditional kimono parade through the town to the accompaniment of shamisen and the Aikawa Ondo folk song.

Kyomachidori in Aikawa

Shukunegi, Niigata Prefecture's only Preservation District for Groups of Traditional Buildings, is a quaint fishermen's village that developed as a port of call for ships sailing the Kitamaebune trade route between Osaka and Hokkaido during the Edo period (1603–1867). Among Shukunegi's 200 or so charming kominka, one of the most striking is a 150-year-old private dwelling named Sankakuya (the Triangular House). The house was originally a square house, but when it was moved to a triangular site on an alleyway, it was rebuilt in a triangular shape, which was quite a bold thing to do. Fortunately, many carpenters in the harbor village were skilled at making the triangular shape of a ship's prow, and so they helped reconfigure the house.

In addition to its history and culture, Sado Island is blessed with a wonderful natural environment. Abundant seafood, rice, sake, and high-grade Sado beef ensure that the island is self-sufficient.

Fall festival in Shukunegi village

Moreover, the islanders are friendly and hospitable. If you are planning a trip to Sado and want to fully enjoy its rich daily life, I recommend a minimum stay of three nights and four days; a week would even be better, if possible. I also recommend riding a bicycle around the island; it's a great way to take in the marvelous scenery and ambience.

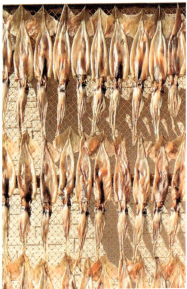

SADO ISLAND
Historic Island
Sado, Niigata

Clockwise from top: Sado's plentiful seafood includes chutoro (tuna), dried squids, and crabs

What to See and Where to Dine and Sleep

RYOTSU OGAWA OUTDOOR WOODBLOCK PRINTS MUSEUM / 大川屋外版画美術館

Printmaking thrives on Sado Island. In the small fishing village of Ryotsu Ogawa, woodblock prints created by villagers on the theme of everyday island life are displayed on the outer walls of kominka throughout the village. The entire village is an outdoor museum where visitors can stroll around appreciating the art.
Ryotsu Ogawa, Sado, Niigata

HANANOKI INN / 御宿 花の木

The 150-year-old kominka inn located near Shukunegi was once a private house that has been relocated and restored. The elegant inn is notable for its hospitable proprietress and delicious meals centering on local fresh fish.
78-1 Shukunegi, Sado, Niigata

YOSABEI GUESTHOUSE / よさべい

Yosabei is a wonderful kominka guesthouse. Built about 200 years ago during the late-Edo period by a former village headman, it has been restored by Karl Bengs, a German architectural designer renowned for his work in revitalizing kominka. I strongly recommend it.
549 Sansegawa, Sado, Niigata

9 MATSUDAI BENGS HOUSE
松代ベンクスハウス
Tokamachi, Niigata

MATSUDAI BENGS HOUSE
Kominka Office and Cafe
2074 Matsudai, Tokamachi, Niigata

The office of Karl Bengs & Associates in Matsudai is in a former Meiji-period ryokan restored by Bengs

A German Architect's Passion for Old Minka Houses

In Tokamachi City, Niigata Prefecture, one of the heaviest snowfall areas in Japan, there are still quite a few thatched houses forming small villages in the hills at elevations of 500 to 2,000 feet. In Taketokoro, one of those villages, Karl Bengs, a German architect, has for the past thirty years devoted his life and talent

88　古民家 ♦ *Kominka*

The landscape around Matsudai-cho (now Tokamachi City)

to preserving the traditional Japanese way of life. As he has said, "When an old house disappears, the spirit and culture that resided within it is also discarded." Bengs will not let that happen, and for that he is a true champion of Japan. He is also a man with a compelling life story.

Bengs was born in Berlin, Germany, in 1942. After World War II, when Germany was divided into East and West, the Bengs family, who lived in the East, became East German citizens. In 1961, just before the Berlin Wall was erected, nineteen-year-old Karl escaped to West Berlin by swimming across the River Spree and passing through barbed wire in search of freedom. He worked as an interior finisher in West Germany, followed by a job in an architectural design firm in Paris. In 1966, inspired by the book *Houses and People of Japan* by architect Bruno Taut (1880–1938), which had belonged to his father, and his interest in karate, Bengs traveled to Japan to study at Nihon University. While he devoted himself to practicing karate, he also visited many Japanese architectural sites, discovering their beauty and technological

Sokakuan, the home of Karl Bengs and his wife, Tina, in Taketokoro

excellence. After seven years of study, he returned to Germany and opened a store in Düsseldorf selling Japanese antiques and antique furniture. At the same time, he began to relocate Japanese private houses and tearooms to various places in Europe, deepening his relationship with kominka. He traveled back and forth between Germany and Japan for this work, and in 1993, at the request of a client who wanted to relocate a private house, he set foot for the first time in Taketokoro in the southern part of Niigata Prefecture. There, he had a fateful encounter with the simple rural landscape of terraced rice paddies scattered in the deep mountains and a kominka. The house was an empty 180-year-old thatched house that looked as if it had been abandoned. However, as he recalls, he found "beauty" in this house. He acquired the land and the house, and began to work on the restoration himself. The result is Sokakuan, Bengs' first kominka restoration in Japan and his and his wife's home to this day. The name Sokakuan—House of Paired Cranes—has a suitably romantic meaning, alluding as it does to a couple who stay together for life, like Karl and Tina.

Sokakuan interior

In the spring of 1998, when I was in charge of a housing information magazine, I heard about this restored kominka. Curious, I visited the house with the intention of reporting on it. I vividly recall my first impression. Sokakuan was different from any of the restored kominka I had previously seen, in more ways than one. Its architectural design could not have been achieved with Japanese sensibilities alone, I thought. I could not help but see that traditional Japanese style and workmanship had been rigorously respected, but there was something else. The restoration exquisitely incorporated a European aesthetic with just the right amount of modernity added. This was a real eye-opener. And when Bengs told me, "Japanese people are throwing away jewelry and buying gravel," I knew exactly what he meant. The notion that wonderful traditional Japanese houses were being allowed to rot and decay in favor of new houses built using soulless prefabricated construction methods really struck a chord with me. Excited by this encounter, I wrote an article about Sokakuan, which was well received. Whether or not it was the catalyst that fired up the kominka revival movement I cannot say, nor would I presume to say, but after it was published, Bengs was interviewed by newspapers, magazines, and TV stations one right after the other. He became a well-known figure in the industry, a celebrity, if you will. At the same time, his business of restoring kominka began to take off. He has now rehabilitated at least sixty kominka, including nine (at last count) in his hometown of Taketokoro and more than thirty others in Niigata Prefecture and the Tokyo metropolitan area, making him one of the most active specialists in this field. His activities to preserve Japan's traditional architecture and revitalize the rural community of Taketokoro and Matsudaicho have received much acclaim, and he has won many awards, including the 2017 Grand Prize in the Prime Minister's Awards for Hometown Development, an honor which he shared with his wife. In addition, programs about Karl and Tina's life in Taketokoro introduced the couple to a wider audience when they were aired on NHK (Japan Broadcasting Corporation) in 2021 and 2022. At the age of eighty-two, my friend Karl is still going strong, and he is determined to complete the restoration of a hundred kominka.

"Old buildings must be taken care of like children," he has said. "If you do not love and care for the building as you would treat a living thing, it will not be reborn. To revitalize a house is to have a philosophy. My work is the restoration of kominka. It is not just a repair job; it is like polishing a gemstone in the rough. I believe that now is the last time to pass on to future generations Japanese culture, technology, and art, which, once lost, will never return."

With passion like this, I do not doubt that Bengs will achieve his goal of 100 revitalized kominka—and then some.

I urge you to visit the wonderful countryside and resilient kominka communities in and around Taketokoro that combine traditional Japanese and European-style design because of Bengs. As you walk around Taketokoro, the exterior colors of the kominka restored by him may surprise you. Red, yellow, and pale pink (the color of Sokakuan) are not usually associated with kominka. But they are in the world of Karl Bengs, whose mentor, Bruno Taut, once wrote, "Color means a joyful existence." And a joyful existence is Bengs' mission in life and work.

⑩ UNNOJUKU
海野宿
Tomi, Nagano

The Town That Never Fails to Enchant

No matter how many times I visit Unnojuku, I am always captivated by the beauty of the townscape.

During the Kamakura period (14th century), Unnojuku flourished as a castle town. Three hundred years later, during the Edo period (17th century), it morphed into a post town on the

UNNOJUKU
Historic Post Town
Tomi, Nagano

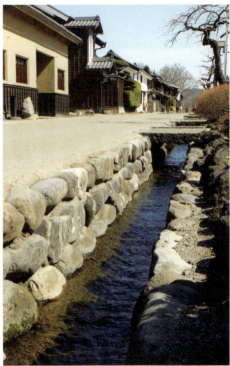

This page, clockwise from top right: A manmade stone stream runs parallel to the highway; willow trees are planted along the waterway; a traditional building in Unnojuku's preservation district. *Opposite page:* Flamboyant udatsu between buildings show off the prestige of the house and help prevent the spread of fire

Hokkoku Kaido highway along which pilgrims traveled to Zenkoji Temple in Nagano and gold was transported from Sado Island to Edo. While there are many old post towns in Japan, Unnojuku with its stately appearance is in a league of its own. Traditional Edo-period inns and thatched-roof kominka line the highway as it passes through Unnojuku; sturdy houses used in the sericulture (silkworm-raising) industry were added during the Meiji period (1868–1912). Distinguishing features include delicate lattice work on many facades, magnificent udatsu (decorative raised wings attached to a roof whose practical purpose is to prevent fire from spreading to neighboring structures), intricate carved designs on second-floor beams, and tower-like mini roofs placed on top of several main roofs to facilitate ventilation. A manmade stone stream carrying clear water runs parallel to the highway; willows planted along the waterway further enhance the charm of Unnojuku, which has been honored as an Important Preservation District for Groups of Traditional Buildings. In my opinion, there is only one thing that would make the atmospheric town even more picture-perfect, and that is if the ronin (wandering samurai) in Akira Kurosawa's classic 1961 film *Yojinbo* were to suddenly appear on its main street. Not even Hollywood could improve on that image.

The Paragon of Kominka Restoration

Karuizawa in Nagano Prefecture—a mountain resort town developed by Westerners in the Meiji period (1868–1912)—is renowned in summer for its cool, fresh air and in autumn for its brilliantly colored foliage. In the area's dense forest, an elegant and majestic kominka stands proudly as a prime example of a properly and sensitively revitalized kominka. Built at the end of the Edo period (1603–1867) in Enzan, Yamanashi Prefecture, the house was moved in 1935 to Karuizawa, where it was named Sangoso (Three Five

SANGOSO &
MINAMIGAOKA ART MUSEUM
三五荘・南ヶ丘美術館
Karuizawa, Nagano

Villa) after the year of its reconstruction. While the exterior of the large building is elegant and majestic, its distinctive thatched gable roof with a raised section along the ridgepole reveals that it was originally a sericulture farmhouse. The raised roof provided necessary ventilation for the breeding of silkworms on the house's upper level. At the time of its renovation as a 20th-century private vacation home, the structure of the house was left as it was when it was first built, but the interior was boldly, if sensitively adapted and remodeled for changing times and lifestyles. However, thanks to the wisdom of its owners and the craftsmanship of the artisans who brought the kominka back to life, certain features were retained, including the thick, shiny black pillars that define the interior space.

The Minamigaoka Art Museum is on the same property as Sangoso and just a short walk away. Small in scale, the museum exhibits excellent works of art, including paintings and pottery. Not to be missed as well is a stroll through the peaceful garden.

SANGOSO & MINAMIGAOKA ART MUSEUM
Historic Kominka and Museum
1052-7 Karuizawa, Kitasaku, Nagano

Opposite, a living room on Sangoso's second floor; *above,* the building's exterior

A Charming Alpine Castle Town

I know Matsumoto like the back of my hand. I spent my schooldays there, and I love every charming corner of what I call my second hometown.

The town at the foot of the Northern Japan Alps is built around the imposing 16th-century Matsumoto Castle, a national treasure, but I'd like to start our tour with a visit to Nakamachi, a row of storehouse-style buildings from the Edo period (1603–1867) on the southern side of the castle. A stroll through this commercial area and its confectioneries, antiques shops, galleries, and restaurants is great fun.

Next, let's head to Nawatedori, a street along the Metoba River, where you can enjoy the fair-like atmosphere every day. Here you will find stores selling antiques and knickknacks. If you get tired from browsing, take a break at Marumo, a coffee shop. Part of an inn dating from the Keio era (1865–68), Marumo is a Matsumoto institution and not to be missed for its

⓬ MATSUMOTO
松本
Matsumoto, Nagano

Marumo Coffee Shop and Inn

古民家 ◆ *Kominka*

Clockwise from top: Matsumoto's Nakamachi district; Matsumoto Folkcraft Museum; the museum's Jizo statue; Matsumoto castle

MATSUMOTO
Historic Castle Town
Matsumoto, Nagano

Marumo Coffee Shop

interior decorated with wooden folk art furniture and designs by Chuo Mingei, a local folkcraft company; the retro atmosphere is comfortable—and the coffee is good. Other kominka that fill their spaces with Matsumoto-made folkcraft furniture include the 130-year-old Hotel Kagetsu and French restaurant Taiman. Feeling inspired to buy a piece or two of folk art furniture for your own home? Then Chuo Mingei's showroom in Nakamachi is the place to go.

Of special interest and just a ten-minute drive from the city center is the Matsumoto Folkcraft Museum. Founded by the late Maruyama Taro, who ran a craft store in Matsumoto, the kominka museum exhibits his personal and eclectic collection of folk art amassed throughout his life. Maruyama's collecting philosophy was simple: He believed that beautiful things have no borders. And so he collected from all regions of Japan as well as from abroad. The collection of approximately 6,000 pieces includes ceramics, glassware, furniture, textiles, and stone Buddhas; exhibits change with the seasons. I am especially fond of the Jizo statue that quietly greets visitors near the museum's entrance. Jizo is a Buddhist deity who protects children and travelers, and I sometimes stop by just to see his face.

Fun fact: Internationally beloved contemporary art star Yayoi Kusama was born in Matsumoto in 1929.

Surviving Against the Odds

The 325-mile-long Nakasendo highway connected Edo (present-day Tokyo) to Kyoto during the Edo period (1603–1867). Of the sixty-eight post towns on this road, Tsumago, which is located in the mountains midway along the route, beautifully preserves the atmosphere of an Edo-period townscape. But its survival wasn't always ensured.

At the end of the Meiji period, around 1911, the Chuo Main Line railroad opened as far as Nagoya. Because the railroad bypassed Tsumago, the town declined and was almost deserted. Worse was still to come. During the postwar high-growth period, Tsumago was threatened with destruction and development. Fortunately, those residents who remained rose up, took

⑬ TSUMAGO
妻籠
Kiso, Nagano

At Matsushiroya, an inn established in 1804, shoji (sliding doors) separate the rooms

matters into their own hands, and enacted their own preservation ordinance. Their principles? "Do not sell, do not rent, do not destroy." Their determination paid off, and they were able to pass on this valuable asset of the Edo period to future generations. Among the many nostalgic charms along Tsumago's half-mile main thoroughfare are rows of kominka with overhanging second floors (dashibari style), wonderful wooden latticework, and plaster-finished fire walls.

It would be a shame to visit Tsumago and not go adventuring outside the town. I recommend a walk along the somewhat steep mountain path of the old Nakasendo road to Magome, a neighboring post town five and a half miles away. For those who are really fit and have time to spare, hiking to Narai, thirty-five miles away, is a challenging option. There are several elegant inns in Tsumago and Magome, but I recommend Koshinzuka 56, a country inn located in a mountain pass in Ohtsumago. Visiting these post towns and staying at this inn will definitely transport you back to the Edo period.

101 Unforgettable Kominka 107

Clockwise from top:
Koshinzuka, a country inn;
Tsumagojuku lantern; a water
mill in Tsumago

TSUMAGO
Historic Post Town
Nagisomachi, Kiso, Nagano

14 YAMANASHI KOMINKA CLUB
山梨古民家倶楽部
Yamanashi

Marufuji Winery

For Love of Kominka

Yamanashi is one of the few prefectures in Japan that is landlocked. But that does not mean it is without appeal. On the contrary. Magnificent Mt. Fuji is in southeastern Yamanashi; there are many hot springs; and Yamanashi's Koshu Valley has been Japan's leading wine region for 150 years, with more wineries than anywhere else in Japan. I'll drink to that—and to the prefecture's many kominka.

In the eastern part of the prefecture, near the Tokyo metropolitan area, several businesses have banded together to form a kind of "club," whose unified purpose is to rediscover, enjoy, and pass on the beauty and charm of traditional Japanese old houses. Currently, the "club" has twelve "members," each of whom owns a repurposed and refurbished kominka. I suggest you visit one or more of these businesses and enjoy a meal, a glass (or two) of wine, some shopping, and a night's lodging in a peaceful kominka setting.

Mt. Fuji watches over the agriculturally productive Koshu Valley

Yamanashi Kominka Club

KATSUNUMA WINERY / 勝沼ワイナリー

This long-established winery, founded in 1937, makes the most of the fertile Koshu Valley's bounty, from grape cultivation to fermentation to bottling of the finished liquid. Katsunuma's motto–"The best, even if it's just one barrel"– expresses the winery's commitment to excellence in viticulture.
371 Iwasaki, Katsunuma, Koshu, Yamanashi

GALLERY NASHIKIBATA / ギャラリー梨木畑

One of the largest kominka in Japan, built in the middle of the Edo period in Minamisanriku-cho, Miyagi Prefecture, has been relocated and preserved, and Japanese sweets are sold in a room in the main building.
1126 Nishihoshimo, Makioka, Yamanashi

GALLERY WA / ギャラリー和

Located in a scenic spot overlooking Mt. Fuji and the Kofu Basin, the gallery is in a restored kominka that was built in Joetsu City, Niigata Prefecture, in the late Meiji period (1911). Paintings, photographs, and old folk tools from the kominka are on display.
484 Somaguchi, Makioka, Yamanashi

Yamanashi Kominka Club

KURAMUBON WINERY / くらむぼんワイン

Before becoming a winery in 1913, the 140-year-old building was a sericulture farmhouse built of hinoki (cypress) without using a single nail. There is an on-site tasting room.
835 Shimoiwasaki, Katsunuma, Koshu, Yamanashi

KORYUEN ORCHARDS / 興隆園

The orchard grows nectarines, which are loved by their many fans for their sweetness and juiciness. Koryuen's reclaimed kominka (actually two old private houses joined together) dates from the late-Meiji (1868–1912) and Taisho (1912–1926) periods, and is at least 110–120 years old.
53-4 Nakamura, Yamanashi, Yamanashi

SATO BUDO / さとうぶどう

The vineyard is located in one of the leading Kyoho grape growing areas in Japan. Its main building is a kominka built at the end of the Meiji period in Joetsu City, Niigata Prefecture, and moved and reconstructed here in 2017.
1984 Nishihoshimo, Makioka, Yamanashi

Left, Gallery Wa; *below,* La Maison Ancienne

YAMANASHI KOMINKA CLUB
Kominka Farms, Wineries, Restaurants, and an Inn
Koshu/Yamanashi, Yamanashi

Yamanashi Kominka Club

SOBAMARU / そば丸

This handmade soba noodle restaurant–housed in a relocated and restored kominka from the Edo period in Niigata Prefecture–is near Erinji, the family temple of Takeda Shingen, a famous 16th-century daimyo (feudal lord) known as the "Tiger of Kai."
1756 Enzanfujiki, Koshu, Yamanashi

HARAMO WINERY / 原茂ワイナリー

The small winery makes wine mainly from Koshu, Yamanashi's world-famous grape. The circa 1870 kominka has been renovated and is now used as a wine store and living space. The popular on-site Cafe Casa da Noma, serving mainly lunch, snacks, and coffee, is open April through November only.
3181 Katsunuma, Koshu, Yamanashi

MARUFUJI WINERY / 丸藤ワイナリー

Japan's oldest winery was founded in 1890 (Meiji 23) by the Omura family, which continues to run it. The building containing the tasting room is a kominka from the late-Edo period (1804–30), which was renovated and revived for the modern age in March 2017.
780 Fujii, Katsunuma, Koshu, Yamanashi

YORO SHUZO / 養老酒造

This small sake brewery in Yamanashi City produces unpasteurized sake the traditional way. The main house, estimated to be more than 200 years old, was built in the style of a village headman's house from the Edo period, with an earthen floor and sunken hearth on the first level; the second level, where the restaurant, Sakagura Kai, is located, was formerly used for sericulture.
567 Kita, Yamanashi, Yamanashi

LA MAISON ANCIENNE / ラ メゾン アンシャンネ

This French restaurant in the Yamanashi wine district is well named. La Maison Ancienne translates as "The Old House," so it is only fitting that it occupies a relocated and restored kominka built about 230 years ago.
5662-5 Kurashina, Makioka, Yamanashi

SUZUKIEN GUESTHOUSE / ワイン民宿鈴木園

The B&B in a kominka dating from around 1870–80 boasts a terrace overlooking vineyards, the Kofu Basin, and the Southern Japan Alps. The renovated rooms are decorated in a blend of Japanese and Western styles.
3284 Katsunuma, Koshu, Yamanashi

⑮ SHIRAKAWAGO & GOKAYAMA
白川郷・五箇山
Gifu and Toyama

UNESCO World Heritage Sites

Gassho-zukuri refers to a style of old house with a pointed rafter roof shaped like two hands joined in prayer ("gassho" is the Buddhist gesture of hands pressed together in greeting or prayer) and finished with straw ropes and vines. Our ancestors, in their wisdom and ingenuity, built these steeply pitched thatched roofs in the neighboring regions of Shirakawago in Gifu Prefecture and Gokayama in Toyama Prefecture, where snowfall is heavy, to prevent snow from accumulating as it would on a flat roof and to provide substantial attic space for sericulture, the raising of silkworms fed on mulberry leaves. Surrounded by high mountains and with only a small amount of cultivated land along the Sho River, sericulture developed as a necessary secondary industry in these areas. Because sericulture requires many laborers, dozens of workers live and work inside large gassho-style houses.

In Gifu Prefecture, Ogimachi is Shirakawago's largest and busiest village, with roughly sixty gassho-style houses clustered together. The compact villages of Ainokura and Suganuma in Toyama Prefecture have fewer traditional farmhouses but are more peaceful. In 1995, UNESCO added the three villages to its list of World Cultural Heritage Sites, praising them for their rarity, authenticity, traditional values, historical importance, and impeccable preservation.

Between Ainokura and Suganuma, two gassho-style buildings are of interest: the Murakami House, an early Edo-period building that has been designated an Important Cultural Property; and an exile hut, a simple one-room structure with neither furniture nor heating to which a samurai outlaw would have been banished in olden times.

Iwase House, the largest five-story gassho-style house in Japan and an Important Cultural Property, is about ten minutes from Suganuma by car. This dignified house, with a shoin-style reception room covered with tatami, was built more than 300 years ago and took eight years to complete.

When I first set foot in this largely unexplored area deep in the mountains about forty years ago, the roads were barely paved, and landslides made them unusable in various places. It was a difficult journey, with many detours along the way. Today, expressways provide easy access to what is now a tourist attraction, with many old gassho-style houses turned into souvenir shops and minshuku (Japanese-style bed and breakfasts). The danger is that Shirakawago and Gokayama could become too popular and too commercial for their own good. For this reason, I have hesitated to include them in this guide. However, these villages contain undeniably important kominka and must be experienced—as long as you know that there are likely to be crowds of sightseers joining you.

OGIMACHI (SHIRAKAWAGO)
Gassho-zukuri Farmhouses
Ohno, Gifu

AINOKURA, SUGANUMA (GOKAYAMA)
Gassho-zukuri Farmhouses
Nanto, Toyama

Clockwise from top: The inside of a gassho-style rafter roof; Gokayama Village; Iwase House is more than 300 years old

HIDA TAKAYAMA & HIDA FURUKAWA
飛騨高山・飛騨古川
Gifu

Towns Built by Master Carpenters

Due to its abundance of high-quality timber, the Hida region in the northern part of Gifu Prefecture has produced skilled carpenters for centuries. In ancient times, carpenters from Hida were called upon to build the capital cities of Nara and Kyoto. Closer to home, these "Hida artisans," as they came to be called, built the towns of Hida Takayama and Hida Furukawa.

HIDA TAKAYAMA & HIDA FURUKAWA
Historic Castle Towns
Hida, Gifu

Clockwise from top left: Kusakabe Folk Museum; exquisite latticework; more than 1,000 carp swim in the Setogawa River in Hida Furukawa

Takayama dates back to 1585, during the Warring States period, when a powerful warlord built Takayama Castle and the surrounding town. There are many things to see in this castle town, but for those who love kominka the best place to start is with a walk along the old streets—Ichinomachi, Ninomachi, and Sannomachi—on the east side of the Miya River that runs north to south through the center of the town. Townhouses line both sides of the narrow streets. Their facades are adorned with beautifully decorated latticework on the first and second floors; their eaves are both uniform and deep; and they are painted with an ancient Japanese mixture of bengara (red iron oxide), pine soot, and persimmon tannin, giving them a charming appearance and atmosphere that is the essence of traditional Japanese architectural beauty. Among the individual buildings, highlights include the Kusakabe Folk Museum with its magnificent beams, built in 1879, and the Yoshijima Residence, a former sake brewer's house with an earthen floor atrium built in 1908. Both are National Important Cultural Properties. To the east of the old houses, a promenade of historic temples invites a stroll.

Hida Furukawa is often referred to as "the backroom of Takayama" because it is quieter than its neighbor. Time permitting, and not too far from Takayama, the Hida Folk Village (Hida no Sato), an outdoor museum of more than thirty kominka from the Edo period (1603–1867) that were transported from Shirakawago and other places in Hida to make up the museum in 1971, is well worth a visit.

Floats in the 400-year-old Furukawa Festival

A Post Town on the Old Tokaido Highway

In ancient times, pedestrians, packhorses, and litters carried by bearers journeyed between Edo (present-day Tokyo) and Kyoto—a distance of approximately 300 miles along the southern coast of Honshu Island—via the Old Tokaido Highway. Fifty-three post towns on this well-maintained, eighteen-foot-wide road provided lodging and sustenance to weary travelers; Sekijuku, built at the end of the 16th century, was the forty-seventh town on the route. Fun fact: Hiroshige's magnificent series of woodblock prints, *Fifty-three Stations of the Tokaido* (1833–34), gives an artist's-eye view of this historic roadway and its post towns.

⟨17⟩ SEKIJUKU
関宿
Kameyama, Mie

Sekijuku's main street

Since its inception, Sekijuku has also been an important transportation hub for pilgrims heading east to the Shinto shrine in Ise and west to Nara's historic eighth-century monuments which are on UNESCO's list of World Heritage Sites. Throughout the Edo period (1603–1867), daimyo (feudal lords) were among the most frequent travelers who passed through Sekijuku because of sankin kotai, a system whereby the lords were required by the controlling shogunate to reside for several months every year in the capital of Edo and the rest of the year in their fiefdoms.

Sekijuku as seen in *Fifty-three Stations of the Tokaido* by Hiroshige

About 200 traditional kominka line both sides of Sekijuku's mile-long main street; many contain antiques stores, sweets shops, and restaurants, among other establishments. It is generally agreed that Sekijuku is one of the best preserved and most atmospheric of the fifty-three post towns along the Old Tokaido Highway, thanks in large part to the efforts of the local population who have worked diligently and tirelessly from early on to preserve the good old things.

SEKIJUKU
Historic Post Town
Kizaki-Nakamachi-Shinjo, Sekimachi,
Kameyama, Mie

⟨18⟩ SANNEIZAKA
産寧坂
Higashiyama, Kyoto

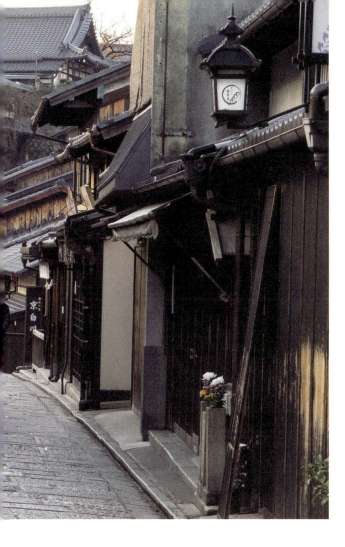

Where Old Kyoto Lives On

The ambience in Kyoto's Higashiyama ward is electric. Here well-preserved traditional wooden buildings with tiled roofs from the Edo, Meiji, Taisho, and Showa eras run up and down narrow cobblestone-paved streets like Sanneizaka (aka Sannenzaka) and Nineizaka (aka Ninenzaka). Shops and restaurants abound—and so do tourists, who flock here in droves during the daytime and

130 古民家 ♦ *Kominka*

Clockwise from top left: Sanneizaka's steep stone steps; Yasaka no tou; the Otowa Waterfall; Kiyomizu-dera, a majestic Buddhist temple and UNESCO World Heritage Site

SANNEIZAKA
Historic Temple Town
2-221, Kiyomizu, Higashiyama, Kyoto

especially on weekends. If you want to experience Old Kyoto at its best—and this is definitely the place to do so—my recommendation is to go early in the morning on weekdays to soak up the atmosphere of Kyoto's machiya (traditional wooden townhouses) in peace and quiet.

Sanneizaka is a slope (zaka translates as "hill"). If you walk along and up it, it will eventually lead you to one of Japan's most majestic Buddhist temples—Kiyomizu-dera, founded in 778 just a few years before Kyoto became the imperial capital of Japan. Dedicated to the worship of the compassionate deity Kannon, Kiyomizu is a historic monument of ancient Kyoto and a UNESCO World Cultural Heritage Site. Legend has it that if you stumble and fall while climbing Sanneizaka's stone steps, you will die within three years. So, be careful.

After enjoying the view of the city from Kiyomizu's massive wooden terrace (often referred to as a "stage"), you can quench your thirst (and more) at Otowa Waterfall. Pure water originating in a spring deep in Mt. Otowa gently flows in three streams to a pavilion just below the temple's terrace. Take one of the cups on offer and dip it into the stream that is said to guarantee success (students about to sit exams invariably choose this one!), or the stream that bestows good fortune in love and romance, or the stream whose water ensures long life. Sip or drink amply, but from one stream only. Drinking from all three is considered greedy, so choose your water wisely and well. And may your wishes come true.

On your way back to Gion, Kyoto's geisha district, and Maruyama Park, where cherry blossoms are the main attraction in early April, you should definitely pass through Ishibekoji. The twisting alley has a great atmosphere and is home to chic restaurants, cafes, and machiya ryokan (traditional townhouse inns) where you can stay overnight and be served breakfast in the morning.

A recommended B&B inn on Ishibekoji:
Uemura 🏠—This inn was started by a former geiko from Gion (in the Kyoto dialect, a geiko is a geisha: literally a "woman of art"). Here, you can enjoy the atmosphere of an Old Kyoto townhouse.

⬥19 MIYAMA TOWN
美山町
Nantan, Kyoto

Dozens of Thatched Kominka

Many kayabuki (traditional thatched houses with steep roofs) still exist in the beautiful rural area of Nantan City in the northern part of Kyoto Prefecture. One of my favorite villages there is Miyama. It is a small residential community of approximately forty-seven kayabuki, of which about twenty were mainly built after the mid-Edo period (18th century). I never tire of looking at its so-called "Kitayama-style" houses and their mountainous backdrop, whether from afar or up close. Since thatched roofs are perishable and need to be repaired as needed and re-thatched (if not completely rebuilt) every five or ten years, Miyama trains young craftsmen in the laborious process. This is a village that takes pride in maintaining its traditions, turning the work of binding layers of pampas grass to a wooden frame into an art form. Thatching is teamwork, and many of Miyama's young apprentices actually live and work in thatched houses the better to hone their thatching skills.

Although Miyama has attracted the lion's share of tourist attention lately, the rustic landscape of nearby Kuta is well worth a visit. Kuta, with kominka dotting the hilly and lush countryside, is like a hidden village, a secret place waiting to be discovered. In late July to August, when Kuta's fields are ablaze with color from the

MIYAMA TOWN
Kominka Farms
Mitamacho, Nantan, Kyoto

Miyama Town, a thatched-roof village

purple chrysanthemums that only grow here, there is no other place like it in Japan.

If you wish to stay in this remote rural area, options include Miyamasou, a first-rate traditional ryokan. Family-run for generations, the inn specializes in cuisine made with edible wild plants, herbs, and mushrooms from the local forests. Large groups and families may want to consider the experience of spending a night under the thatched roof of one of Miyama's "futon and breakfasts."

136

 INE TOWN
伊根町
Yosa, Kyoto

A Unique Waterfront Settlement

Ine, a picturesque fishing town on the Tango Peninsula in Kyoto Prefecture, is known for its more than 200 funaya (boathouses) built around a semicircular bay. The wooden structures—one right next to the other with hardly any space in between them—are uniform in appearance. The gable ends all face the sea, and

138　古民家 ♦ *Kominka*

Ine Bay

each house has two floors. The first floor opens directly on to the water and is where fishing boats are launched, landed, and safely stored (think of it as a garage for a boat instead of a car). The first level also serves as a workspace where fishermen maintain their equipment and dry and store the fish they have caught. They and their families live upstairs, on the second floor. For a panoramic view of just how special Ine's funaya are, a sightseeing boat tour is recommended. From a distance, the houses look as if they float on the water.

　I first visited Ine about thirty years ago. At that time, only one or two boathouses were being used as guesthouses, and I was fortunate enough to stay at one of them while taking photographs and walking around the town. Today, more people visit Ine, and there are more places in which to stay. But Ine has definitely not become a tourist trap. It is still a working town whose atmosphere and traditional way of life have been preserved, and that pleases me.

Top, left and right, this brewery is said to be over 240 years old; *bottom,* Ine's boathouses

INE TOWN
Historic Fishermen's Village
Yosa, Kyoto

21 TAMBA SASAYAMA & HOTEL NIPPONIA
丹波篠山・ホテルニッポニア
Hyogo

Sasayama's merchant district

A Castle Town Turned Into a Hotel

Located not too far from the Keihanshin metropolitan area, the city of Tamba Sasayama lies in a basin surrounded on all sides by mountains and exquisite rural scenery. Historically, the city began as a castle town when Sasayama Castle was built approximately 400 years ago in the early Edo period. Today, the ruins of the strategically placed fortress are at the heart of the

古民家 ◆ *Kominka*

Clockwise from top: The front desk of the Sasayama Castle Town Hotel Nipponia is in the Onae kominka; preserved earthen floor and antique kamado (cooking stove), also in Onae; Nipponia's Yomena villa, a renovated merchant house, is more than 100 years old; a Nipponia guest room

preservation area, which includes the old samurai and the old merchant quarters that still encircle the castle as they did in ancient times. In the old samurai part of town, the row-house gate of a high-ranking samurai lies opposite the outer moat of the castle; to the west of the castle, samurai residences with thatched hip and gable roofs, earthen walls, and roofed gates face the street. The old merchant town consists of beautiful rows of townhouses built between the late-Edo period (mid–19th century) and the Taisho period (early 20th century). Many of these kominka have been converted into restaurants and stores. All told, the preservation area encompasses 100 acres, measuring approximately 5,000 feet east to west and 2,000 feet north to south—the perfect size for a leisurely walk and daylong excursion. But why not extend your visit to this kominka town and stay at one of Japan's most distinctive hotels, the Sasayama Castle Town Hotel Nipponia?

Nipponia is a luxury hotel brand whose concept and mission is to renovate traditional old buildings throughout Japan and convert them into lodgings where visitors can experience local history, culture, and lifestyle. The Nipponia hotel in Sasayama is a decentralized hotel because it consists of not one building but eight kominka scattered throughout the town. For example, guests can choose to stay in a former bank owner's residence built in the early Meiji period, or in a former geisha house, or in a townhouse built at the end of the Edo period. Unlike other hoteliers who in recent years have modernized kominka without fully understanding the cultural and technical merits of the old buildings, Nipponia respects the historicity of the original buildings without in any way spoiling their authentic charm and atmosphere.

TAMBA SASAYAMA
Historic Castle Town
Hyogo

HOTEL NIPPONIA
25 Nishimachi, Tanbasasayama, Hyogo

The Most Kominka in Japan

In Japan, where scrap-and-build is unfortunately a recurring theme today, Imaicho is the exception. It steadfastly holds on to the atmosphere of the Warring States and Edo periods.

Initially, it was a temple town, built by followers of the Jodo Shinshu sect of Buddhism in the middle of the 16th century. The sect's Shounenji temple still stands proudly in the town's center. During Japan's turbulent

22 IMAICHO
今井町
Kashihara, Nara

146　古民家 ♦ *Kominka*

Top, kominka line Imaicho's streets; *bottom,* the remains of protective moats set up during the Warring States period (1467–1568)

Warring States period of civil wars, a moat helped protect Imaicho from destruction. When peace was restored, autonomy as an independent, self-governing entity followed, and Imaicho prospered as a merchant town during the Edo period, thanks in large measure to commerce and trade with the port cities of Osaka and Sakai. The area is notable today for its large number of national, prefectural, and city-designated cultural properties—and its kominka.

Approximately 500 traditional wooden structures line Imaicho's streets, making this the largest architectural preservation area in Japan. Nowhere else have this many kominka survived on such a large scale and in one locale. I do not exaggerate when I say that Imaicho is a miracle.

Detail of an antique Japanese yoke

IMAICHO
Historic Temple Town
Kashihara, Nara

Beautiful Canals, Historic Warehouses

Kurashiki's name says it all: This is a city of warehouses (kura). During the Edo period (1603–1867), when the city was under the direct control of the shogunate, it developed as an important inland port for the storage and distribution of rice, the area's most valuable agricultural product. Because the shogunate granted autonomy to Kurashiki's merchants and gave them preferential treatment, the town prospered and

23 KURASHIKI
倉敷
Okayama

Kurashiki's scenic Bikan Historical Quarter

the population swelled. Rice was brought to Kurashiki where it was temporarily kept in warehouses before being shipped to Osaka and Edo. Canals were specially built within the city on which boats could easily transport their cargo from the warehouses, with their distinctive white walls and black tiles, to the port. Warehouses and a section of the canal system have been preserved in the scenic Bikan Historical Quarter, where weeping willow trees overhang the canal and bridges cross the water.

    I have visited Kurashiki many times, and each time I return, I get the impression that the preservation area is expanding and improving in the right direction. However, the number of souvenir stores and restaurants in the backstreets of this popular traditional townscape has increased, and uncontrolled signs and billboards are beginning to spoil the scene. That said, Kurashiki is still a good place to visit.

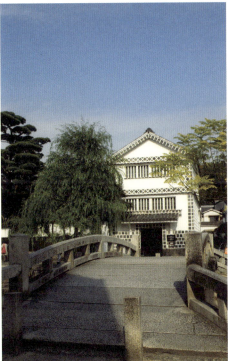

Clockwise from top: Ivy Square, former site of a textile factory, now contains a hotel and stores; Ohara Museum of Art, whose abundant collections of folk art are of extremely high quality; a bridge crosses a canal in the Bikan Historical Quarter

KURASHIKI
Historic Port Town
Okayama

㉔ FUKIYA
吹屋
Takahashi, Okayama

The Hirokane merchant family used their fortune from manufacturing bengara to build a castle-like residence at the end of the Edo period

Birthplace of Japan Red

After about an hour's drive into the mountains from Japan Railways Takahashi Station, you come upon an extraordinary sight: a stately red townscape. Buildings with distinctive roofs made of reddish-bronze Sekishu clay tiles and exterior walls uniformly painted red glint in the sunlight. This is the village of Bitchu Fukiya.

Fukiya Village (1986)

Originally developed around a copper mine, Fukiya flourished as a major producer of bengara (red iron oxide) from the end of the Edo period through the Meiji period. Bengara is a pigment used to paint porcelain, lacquerware, and the exterior walls of shrines, temples, and residences, and is called "Japan red" because of its unique color.

Wealthy merchants who made their fortunes from bengara built the community of Fukiya, but they did so in a very un-Japanese way. Rather than build lavish mansions that reflected their individuality and therefore were different from each other, they grouped together and invited master carpenters to build the entire town under a unified concept. This is a truly unique process in Japan.

In addition to preserving its distinctive architecture, Fukiya ensures that its culture is also preserved through such events as Bitchu Kagura (Shinto music and dance performances) and the annual Bengara Lantern Festival. It should come as no surprise that this beautiful, one-of-a-kind village is listed as an Important Preservation District for Groups of Traditional Buildings.

101 Unforgettable Kominka 155

Clockwise from top; The main street of Fukiya Village; Fukiya post office; roofs with Sekishu clay tiles

FUKIYA
Historic Mining Town
Takahashi, Okayama

Ryokan Architecture at Its Finest

I have traveled all over the world, staying at a variety of inns. Someday I hope to compile a book of my favorites. Sekitei in Hiroshima Prefecture will definitely be in my Top Ten. While it is not a kominka—yet—it is an inn where the best of Japanese ryokan architecture in all its various forms is concentrated to be seen, appreciated, and enjoyed by guests from Japan and abroad.

 SEKITEI
石亭
Hatsukaichi, Hiroshima

At Sekitei ryokan, a former tea ceremony room has been converted into a bathroom

古民家 ◆ *Kominka*

SEKITEI
Kominka Inn
*3-5-27 Miyahama-Onsen,
Hatsukaichi, Hiroshima*

Sekitei ryokan offers twelve accommodations (most are in separate buildings) surrounding a serene garden; each has its own name, high-quality design, and superb decor. The overall effect is like that of a small, secluded community of private residences nestled together. Guests can expect to feel the cozy comfort of being cocooned in their own individually tailored retreat. Perhaps this is due to the inn's owner being a hobbyist builder, who joyfully has constructed each element in collaboration with architects and skilled carpenters. As someone who also enjoys building houses, I am in total sympathy with him and his achievement.

I have visited Sekitei several times, and each time I have enjoyed a different experience. Once, I stayed in "Anan," the former private study of the owner. On another visit, I stayed in "Kochuan" where, to my surprise, the former tea ceremony room had unexpectedly been turned into a bathroom with a large tub in its center! Not only is the hotel's concept wonderful, but the food and the hospitality of the staff are also first-rate.

Although Sekitei is young compared to the kominka in this book—its main building dates from about fifty-eight years ago— it is getting older very year! In twenty, thirty, and fifty years, Sekitei will be even more attractive and valuable as one of Japan's traditional "old" hideaways.

26 HAGI
萩
Yamaguchi

A Typical Castle Town

Many of Japan's major cities started out as castle towns in the early modern period (mid–16th century to mid–19th century), but most of them have unfortunately lost their old appearance due to rapid modernization and the ravages of war. Hagi is an exception.

The castle around which Hagi grew was built in 1604 by the powerful Mori samurai clan that ruled the feudal Choshu domain in the Chugoku region. When the Meiji Restoration in 1868 put an end to the feudal system of government, castle fortresses throughout Japan were disassembled, including Hagi Castle in 1874. While the castle lies in ruins in a handsome park setting which is open to the public, the layout, composition, and scale of Hagi City and its streets still retain the look and feel of a typical castle town. One reason may be that Hagi's geographical location—surrounded by mountains on three sides with the Sea of Japan on the fourth—isolated it from modernization.

Hagi has no fewer than four Important Preservation Districts for Groups of Traditional Buildings, whose original states have been carefully conserved. The Hamasaki district contains merchant quarters and a port which tell the story of the role Hagi played

Hagi's Hamasaki district

as a center of transportation, trade, fishing, and boat building. The earthen walls of more than a hundred traditional townhouses and storehouses are especially notable; the unmistakable crisscross pattern of black tile and white plaster indicates a merchant's status and wealth within the community. There are samurai mansions and residences in the Horiuchi district and the smaller Hiyako district. In the suburbs, about twelve miles from the city center, Sasanamiichi is a post town that resembles a rural farming village where remnants of the old highway still exist. When these preservation areas are viewed together, the historical and traditional aspects of Hagi as a castle town can be understood in a multilayered and comprehensive manner.

Fun fact: Kikugahama, a white-sand beach minutes from Hagi Castle, is a relaxing place to take a break from sightseeing.

HAGI
Historic Castle Town
Yamaguchi

27 SOTODOMARI
外泊
Ainan, Ehime

Living Culture Protected by Stone Walls

Sotodomari is a village located in a small bay on a peninsula which juts out from the southwestern edge of Ainan in the Minamiuwa district on Shikoku, the smallest of Japan's four main islands. About fifty houses—each surrounded by tall stone walls—climb in a cluster from the waterfront to midway up a steep

mountain slope. This one-of-a-kind landscape has earned the village the nickname Ishigaki no Sato (Village of Stone Walls). The stone walls protect the houses from high tides, typhoons, and monsoons; and some of them reach as high as the eaves of the houses. The construction of the compound and the building of the stone walls were all done by the residents between the end of the Edo period and the beginning of the Meiji period (1868–1912); maintenance continues to be performed by the residents today. The main industry of Sotodomari is fishing. The kitchen of each house is strategically located on the seaward side of the house so that the women can watch the men fish while they do their chores. The stone walls in front of the kitchen windows are designed to be slightly lower so that the women can see farther out to sea and thereby keep a close eye on the men at work, hoping for a large catch of the day and praying for their safe return home. I never tire of looking down from the top of the mountain at the beautifully piled-up stone walls and fortresslike village. It is a wonderful sight.

SOTODOMARI
Historic Fishermen's Village
Minami-uwa, Ainan, Ehime

28 UCHIKO
内子
Kita, Ehime

Above right, Honhaga family residence on Uchiko's main street

Wealthy Wax Merchants Lived Here

Uchiko is a town that has long flourished as a transportation hub and a transit point for the centuries-old Shikoku Pilgrimage, the 745-mile circular route around the island of Shikoku featuring stops at eighty-eight Buddhist temples. Commercially, from the Edo period to the Meiji period, Uchiko

Top, Uchiko's main street; *bottom,* kote-e plaster reliefs decorate rich merchants' residences

prospered as a center for paper and wax production, most notably high-quality mokuro wax, a substance derived from the berries of sumac trees native to Japan and used in candles. At its peak, Uchiko accounted for about thirty percent of Japan's total production of the wax. But in the modern era, oil and electricity replaced wax as fuel, and wax production in Uchiko declined. Fortunately, the town's preserved Yokaichi district and its traditional townhouses and residences of rich merchants look as they did a hundred years ago and bear witness to the wealth and prosperity of the old days.

The main street of Yokaichi is approximately 2,000 feet long, and on both sides there are large dwellings, including the Omura Residence (built between 1789 and 1801), one of the oldest buildings in the town. The Machiya Museum (built in 1793) is a valuable cultural asset, as it is an old townhouse that predates wax production in Uchiko; the typical merchant house's inner living room, indigo warehouse, and other annexed buildings are open to the public. The main house of the Honhaga family, which made its fortune from wax, was built in 1889 (Meiji 22) and is truly impressive. The stately building is decorated with kote-e plaster reliefs, onigawara roof ornaments, and geometric namako tile walls; a wax museum is on the premises. Fun fact: Uchiko wax achieved international prominence when the Honhaga family displayed their goods at the 1900 Exposition Universelle in Paris.

During the daytime, Uchiko is crowded with tourists, but after the tourists leave in the evening, the town regains its serenity. Although a small town, it is worth staying overnight to relish the peace and quiet in the morning and evening.

UCHIKO
Historic Merchant Town
Kita, Ehime

29 KIRAGAWA
吉良川
Muroto, Kochi

Kominka Built to Withstand Wind and Rain

As you drive north from Cape Muroto on the west side of the Muroto Peninsula on the island of Shikoku, you will see rows of old houses with distinctive plaster walls, gabled roofs, and stone walls made of rounded stones. This is the town of Kiragawa, an Important Preservation District for Groups of Traditional Buildings.

Since ancient times, Kiragawa has prospered as a center for forest resources such as lumber and firewood and, after the Meiji period (1868–1912), as a producer of high-quality binchotan charcoal. But it is other natural materials that account for Kiragawa's unique appearance. Typhoons have always plagued the town, whose geographical location makes it particularly vulnerable to damage from violent gusts of wind and heavy downpours of rain. Protecting homes (mostly built in the Meiji and Tasho periods) and livelihoods from such damage is of the utmost importance and therefore the town's architecture reflects that concern. The first thing that catches the eye is the masonry. The walls of every house are built with round, disk-shaped stones piled up in a regular pattern. If you go to the nearby seashore, you will find that the stones there are all round, with no corners. The rough waves cause the stones to collide with each other, naturally creating their perfectly round shape. These are the stones that were transported to the town for the buildings' walls, many of which were then slathered and sealed with pure white Taso plaster for waterproofing. These thick stone walls in combination with special tile eaves is genius, and a perfect example of the wisdom inherent in constructing kominka that are rationally adapted to the local climate. Surprisingly, Kiragawa has yet to become a tourist attraction. All the better for you to enjoy a leisurely stroll around the Shimomachi district near the coast and the Kamimachi district on the mountain side, where you can experience ordinary life without interference. If you have time, you may want to extend your visit to the neighboring town of Aki.

KURAKUKAN KURAJUKU 蔵空間蔵宿
Located in a corner of the Important Preservation District, this 120-year-old rice warehouse has been renovated into a cafe with overnight accommodations. If guests are lucky, the owner and his wife will entertain with a guitar and piano duet.
2234 Ko, Kiragawa, Muroto, Kochi

101 Unforgettable Kominka 175

Left, white Tosa plaster and round stones; *right and below,* Kurakukan Kurajuku

KIRAGAWA
Historic Town
Kiragawa, Muroto, Kochi

A Sandwich-shaped Castle Town

At the southern tip of Kunisaki Peninsula on the island of Kyushu, there is a small but wonderful town called Kitsuki, an authentically atmospheric reminder of the Edo period (1603–1867). In the Meiji period (late-19th century), the residents of the town emphatically said no to "progress" and refused to allow the railroad to run through their town; so a rail station was built in the suburbs some distance away. As a result,

30 KITSUKI
杵築
Oita

the old town preserved its traditional ways while the area around the station was developed and became a run-of-the-mill local town without any distinguishing characteristics or noteworthy attractions. Is there really any reason to visit the new town? On the other hand, the old town attracts a lot of attention in this modern age. Call it an irony of history.

Kitsuki is a castle town whose centerpiece, Kitsuki Castle, dates from 1394 during the Muromachi period. But what makes Kitsuki so attractive and unusual is its shape. A road runs east to west through the town, and two plateaus, one north and one south, flank the road. Residences of senior samurai warriors and their chief retainers are on both plateaus; merchant houses are in the valley between the plateaus. The town looks like a sandwich and thus it is known as the "sandwich-shaped castle town." More than that, it is the only sandwich-shaped castle town in Japan and therefore an Important Preservation District for Groups of Traditional Buildings.

There are many traditional towns with long histories on Kyushu, but the topography and ambience of Kitsuki set it apart from the rest. However, there are no hotels in Kitsuki. You can stay in nearby Beppu Onsen or Yufuin, where you can rent a car for a day trip.

Merchant houses

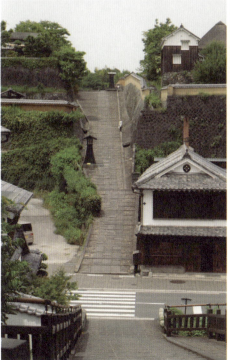

Clockwise from top: The Ohara residence (samurai house); Kanjoba-no-saka slope; Suya-no-saka slope

KITSUKI
Historic Castle Town
Oita

31 SANSOU MURATA
山荘無量塔
Yufuin, Oita

One of the Finest Kominka Inns in Japan

I have stayed at many kominka inns throughout Japan, but Sansou Murata in Yufuin is one of the most impressive and creative. It is a relatively new ryokan, built and opened in 1992, but everything about it is old, beginning with its concept of taking a centuries-old kominka and revitalizing it for modern-day hospitality. Make that a dozen kominka. Murata's founder and his architect visited Niigata Prefecture many times in search of kominka for their inn; eventually they found twelve, ranging in age from 100 to 200 years old, and moved them to Oita Prefecture, where they were rebuilt and restored to create this luxurious hot springs retreat. The detached cottages, each with a different design and character enhanced by bold decorations, sit on four acres at the base of a mountain. The separate main building—a restored Meiji-period (1868–1912) kominka—is stately, stylish, and very comfortable; it houses the lobby, dining area, and Tan's Bar. A huge movie-theater speaker painted burgundy takes pride of place in Tan's Bar. Tannoy speakers, a favorite of the founder, who was an audiophile, are

also on display and in use. Relaxing over a drink while listening to classical music or jazz played through these speakers is just one of many moments of pleasure offered by Sansou Murata.

Yufuin used to be a hot springs resort town with a sedate, rustic atmosphere, but if you expect that now, you may be disappointed. It has become a trendy modern resort town much favored by the young. In spite of this, Sansou Murata is worth a visit for those who want to experience a truly authentic kominka inn. After the founder's untimely death at a young age, the manager and about seventy staff members have worked hard to make it one of the best ryokan in Japan, receiving high praise from both domestic and international guests.

SANSOU MURATA
Kominka Inn
1264-2 Yufuin, Kawakami, Yufu, Oita

🔷32 TAKETOMI ISLAND
竹富島
Yaeyama, Okinawa

Japan's Southernmost Subtropical Island

Japan is an archipelago composed of approximately 7,000 islands. Of the dozens of small islands in Okinawa Prefecture, Japan's southernmost and westernmost prefecture, Taketomi in the remote Yaeyama Islands takes exceptional pride in its traditional way of life. A low island made of Ryukyu limestone created by

古民家 ♦ *Kominka*

Clockwise from top: A traditional wood house; a shisa, a traditional Okinawan folk sculpture of a fanged beast, sits on a roof to ward off evil; a fun way to travel from Iriomote Island to Yubu Island near Taketomi is to go by buffalo cart through the shallows; coral stone wall

the uplift of the coral reefs that surround it, Taketomi is oval-shaped and flat; its circumference is little more than five and a half miles—just the right size for a day trip from nearby Ishigaki Island. Blessed with a subtropical climate and beautiful beaches, this Important Preservation District for Groups of Traditional Buildings boasts traditional one-story wood houses topped with red-tile hipped roofs and enclosed by stone walls. At the village's entrance, there is a square called Sunmasha, where a large banyan tree with stones heaped around it divides the white sandy road. Based on Feng Shui philosophy, this is to protect the village and island from demons and diseases entering from outside. Protection is key to the preservation of the kominka that are special to this region. The Taketomi Island Charter insists on five basic principles: "Do not sell, do not pollute, do not disturb, do not destroy, and utilize traditional culture and the natural landscape as tourism resources." It also states: (1) When building new, enlarging, or repairing buildings, the traditional style should be followed. (2) The enclosure around the house should be made of coral limestone piled on the ground. (3) When buying or selling real estate, or when building new, enlarging, remodeling, or demolishing buildings, the community center and the coordinating committee must be notified in advance. An autonomous organization has been established, and the islanders are directly involved in efforts to respect and preserve the island's environment, history, and culture for themselves, future generations, and visitors who choose to come here.

TAKETOMI ISLAND
Historic Town
Taketomi, Yaeyama, Okinawa

MORE GREAT CHOICES

- ㉝ Hakodate Motomachi 函館元町
- ㉞ Otaru Canal 小樽運河
- ㉟ Kuroyu Onsen Inn 黒湯温泉
- ㊱ Tateiwa Village 舘岩村
- ㊲ Kitakata 喜多方
- ㊳ Tochigi 栃木
- ㊴ Kawagoe 川越
- ㊵ Chinryuso Kyotei 枕流荘 京亭
- ㊶ Japan Folk Crafts Museum 日本民藝館
- ㊷ Kagurazaka 神楽坂
- ㊸ Toutouan 燈々庵
- ㊹ Hinode Sanso 日の出山荘
- ㊺ Buaiso 武相荘
- ㊻ Iida Family Residence 飯田家住宅
- ㊼ Oginoshima Village 荻ノ島
- ㊽ Sankyoson 散居村
- ㊾ Kanazawa 金沢
- ㊿ Kumagawajuku 熊川宿

- ◆51 Obama Nishigumi 小浜西組
- ◆52 Oshino Village 忍野村
- ◆53 Aoni 青鬼
- ◆54 Obuse 小布施
- ◆55 Naraijuku 奈良井宿
- ◆56 Koshinzuka こうしんづか
- ◆57 Mugeiso 無藝荘
- ◆58 Kasenan Seni Onsen Iwanoyu 花仙庵 仙仁温泉 岩の湯
- ◆59 Gero Onsen Yunoshimakan 下呂温泉 湯之島館
- ◆60 Mino 美濃
- ◆61 Numazu Club 沼津倶楽部
- ◆62 Izu Matsuzaki 伊豆 松崎
- ◆63 Kakujoro 角上楼
- ◆64 Arimatsu 有松
- ◆65 Asuke 足助
- ◆66 Shiratama 志ら玉
- ◆67 Sakamoto 坂本
- ◆68 Omihachiman 近江八幡

- ㊾ Hotel Koo Otsu Hyakucho ホテル講 大津百町
- ㋀ Gion Shinbashi 祇園新橋
- ㋁ Sagatoriimoto 嵯峨鳥居本
- ㋂ Ishibekoji 石塀小路
- ㋃ Tawaraya 俵屋
- ㋄ Mo-an 茂庵
- ㋅ Kamishichiken 上七軒
- ㋆ Hirakatashuku 枚方宿
- ㋇ Takenaka Carpentry Tools Museum 竹中大工道具館
- ㋈ Tatsuno 龍野
- ㋉ Izushi 出石
- ㋊ Gose 御所
- ㋋ Ouda 大宇陀
- ㊑ Ryujin Onsen Kamigoten 龍神温泉 上御殿
- ㊒ Kurayoshi 倉吉
- ㊓ Misasa Onsen 三朝温泉
- ㊔ Matsue 松江
- ㊕ Omori Iwami Ginzan 大森 石見銀山

- ⑧⑦ Takahashi 高梁
- ⑧⑧ Tomonoura 鞆の浦
- ⑧⑨ Onomichi 尾道
- ⑨⓪ Ryokan Onomichi Nishiyama 旅館 尾道西山
- ⑨① Wakimachi Minamimachi 脇町南町
- ⑨② Kasashima Town 笠島
- ⑨③ Shimayado Mari 島宿真里
- ⑨④ Yusuhara 梼原
- ⑨⑤ Yanagawa 柳川
- ⑨⑥ Tachibana-tei Ohana 立花邸 御花
- ⑨⑦ Takegawara Onsen 竹瓦温泉
  Dogo Onsen Honkan 道後温泉本館
  Katakurakan 片倉館
- ⑨⑧ Usuki 臼杵
- ⑨⑨ Gajoen 雅叙苑
- ⑩⓪ Izumifumoto 出水麓
- ⑩① Chiran 知覧

33 Hakodate Motomachi 函館元町 / Hokkaido

Japan's isolation from the outside world during the Edo period (1603–1867) ended in 1853 when Commodore Matthew Perry of the United States Navy sailed into Edo Bay (today's Tokyo Bay). His goal? To establish diplomatic relations and to open Japanese ports to trade with the United States. In 1859, Hakodate became one of Japan's first international trading centers, welcoming ships from the West, Russia, and China. Hakodate's Motomachi district overlooking Hakodate Bay is a striking townscape, with an architectural and cultural mix of traditional Japanese and Western-style residences and places of worship.

34 Otaru Canal 小樽運河 / Hokkaido

Otaru Canal is one of Hokkaido Prefecture's most popular tourist attractions. But that wasn't always the case. In the 1960s, the canal and the warehouses from the Meiji period that lined it were scheduled for demolition to make way for yet another motorway to join others that were then sweeping through the area. Fortunately, concerned citizens of the city of Otaru launched a twenty-year campaign that resulted in preserving a portion of the canal and its warehouses, which are now museums, shops, and restaurants. If all of the canal had been destroyed, as proposed, Otaru would have become a nondescript provincial city instead of the bustling port town it is today.

35 Kuroyu Onsen Inn 黒湯温泉 / Senboku, Akita

Of the seven or so hot springs in Nyuto Onsen village, the oldest and most famous is Tsurunoyu. But, if you are feeling adventurous, there is an off-the-beaten-path gem just a few kilometers down an unpaved road in a secluded valley. This is Kuroyu, an inn whose several kominka with thatched roofs—some as old as 350 years—surround a therapeutic, bubbling hot spring which emits white steam and the scent of sulfur. The thatched house in the photo was built for the Japanese imperial family when they visited for spring skiing in 1964; four to five people can now rent it out and prepare their own meals in the house's kitchenette.

36 Tateiwa Village 館岩村 / Fukushima

Tateiwa Village is located on a plateau surrounded by mountains in the southwestern corner of Fukushima Prefecture. Since this is a heavy snowfall area, beginning at the end of the 16th century, the people of Maezawa hamlet have adapted the architecture of their homes to suit the harsh climate. Large L-shaped thatched-roof houses have long corridors that stretch from the main road to the living quarters which are set back from the road. In winter, they and their livestock (because of the weather, horses are kept indoors rather than in an open-air pen) can easily access the road without shoveling mounds of snow. The nearby community of Mizuhiki hamlet has a cluster of similar thatched-roof houses set in rice paddies. The well-maintained old houses create a beautiful traditional landscape.

37 Kitakata 喜多方 / Fukushima

No other town in Japan is like Kitakata, set in the rich countryside in the northern part of the Aizu Basin. Here, there are thousands of traditional fireproof kura (warehouses)—the number could be as high as 4,000 in the town and its vicinity—dating from the Edo and Meiji periods. In the old days, Kitakata's prosperous merchants safely stored their treasures in these kura; today, many of them have been repurposed as shops, sake and miso breweries, tatami rooms, temples, inns, art galleries, coffeehouses, and restaurants. It is said that there are more ramen restaurants per capita in Kitakata than anywhere else in Japan, so bring your appetite.

38 Tochigi 栃木 / Tochigi

Tochigi's location on the Uzuma River has served it well throughout its history, first as a castle town (the castle was built around 1591) and afterward as an Edo-period commercial hub. A 400-foot-long stretch of 18th- and 19th-century merchant houses and warehouses along the river bear witness to the prosperous past, and include that of the Tsukada family of lumber wholesalers. Also of interest in Tochigi is Okada Kinenkan (Okada Memorial Hall), the residence of the prominent Okada family since 1688. The colorful Tochigi Float Festival is held every two years in November. If your visit does not coincide with the traditional street festival, you can still soak up its atmosphere at the Dashi Kaikan, where floats (dashi) and a video of the festival are on exhibit.

39. Kawagoe 川越 / Saitama

The city of Kawagoe is less than an hour from Tokyo. Originally a castle town, Kawagoe thrived in the Edo period (1603–1867) as a center for the distribution of goods to the city of Edo, as Tokyo was then called. Trade between the two cities was so good, Kawagoe earned the nickname "Koedo," which means "Little Edo." Kawagoe's Warehouse District (Kurazukuri) from that era is a must-visit. Its twenty or so warehouses are traditional, but they are not made of wood. Instead, they are constructed of layers of fire-resistant clay, just like the Osawa Family Residence, a National Important Cultural Property which survived Kawagoe's Great Fire of 1893.

40 Chinryuso Kyotei 枕流荘 京亭 / Yorii, Saitama

Kyotei, located on the banks of the Arakawa River, is a kappo ryokan, an inn that serves food—with a difference. "Kappo" means "cutting and cooking" but unlike in a restaurant where guests do not see the chef at work, "kappo" is performed at a table around which guests sit and watch the chef prepare their meal. The inn is famous for its ayu (sweetfish) cuisine. The tastefully designed old house took five years to build and was the retreat of composer and lyricist Sassa Koka (1886–1961), who drew up the plans himself. Only two couples can stay at the hotel at one time. Make a reservation here, and you will experience a special night and forget about time.

㊶ Japan Folk Crafts Museum 日本民藝館 / Komaba, Tokyo

In Japan, "kominka" and "mingei" are closely connected. "Mingei" refers to folk crafts made by unknown artisans, and therefore a traditional Japanese old house is itself a piece of mingei (folk) art. Philosopher and art critic Yanagi Muneyoshi (1889–1961), also known as Soetsu Yanagi, recognized the beauty of everyday items and founded the Mingei Movement. He researched and collected handicrafts from all over Japan, establishing the Japan Folk Crafts Museum in 1936. The wooden building is of traditional Japanese design, but incorporates Western touches throughout. The museum's collection consists of approximately 17,000 items.

㊷ Kagurazaka 神楽坂 / Shinjuku, Tokyo

Tokyo is a sprawling, helter-skelter modern metropolis with buildings that stand check by jowl. But within the densely packed city, several charming human-scale neighborhoods beckon. One such is Kagurazaka from the Edo period (1603–1867), a former geisha and entertainment district. Kagura refers to ritualistic music dedicated to the gods and played to motivate worshippers as they climb the steep zaka (hill/slope) on which the neighborhood is located, carrying portable shrines during festivals. The area's narrow stone streets twist and turn and are fun to walk along, even get lost along. Some have amusing names, like Kakurenbo Yokocho (Hide and Seek Alley). Fashionable shops and restaurants, notably French, abound.

43 Toutouan 燈々庵 / Akiruno, Tokyo

Talented restaurateur Kenji Takamizu has revitalized a rice storehouse—once owned by a village headman and passed down through seventeen generations since the Edo period (1603–1867)—into a traditional Japanese kaiseki restaurant and gallery. Kaiseki, universally recognized as Japan's haute cuisine, refers to a leisurely and artfully prepared and presented multicourse meal of small dishes. While kaiseki restaurants can be found all over Japan, Toutouan is a pioneer of its kind and a champion of regional ingredients and cooking. The food is delicious, and so is the decor which joins traditional Japanese aesthetics to a modern sense of style.

44 Hinode Sanso 日の出山荘 / Tama, Tokyo

Of all past US presidents, Ronald Reagan was the one who truly experienced a kominka. During Reagan's state visit to Japan in November 1983, Prime Minister Yasuhiro Nakasone invited the president to Hinode Sanso, his private retreat located in the mountains about forty miles west of central Tokyo, for a taste of Japanese culture, hospitality, and diplomacy. Reagan described the kominka in his diary as "a tiny, typical Japanese house where we sat on the floor & had a real Japanese lunch." The thatched-roof kominka, a rustic farmhouse built in the late-Edo period (ca. 1850), memorializes the summit between the two leaders and is open to the public.

◆45 Buaiso 武相荘 / Machida, Tokyo

East meets West in Buaiso, a thatched-roof, wooden farmhouse in the city of Machida. The kominka is the former home of distinguished postwar bureaucrat Jiro Shirasu (1902–1985) and his wife, Masako (1910–1998), an equally distinguished author, art and antiques connoisseur, and collector. Together, they collaborated on a house that married their sensibilities: Cambridge University-educated Jiro's love of English country life and Masako's deep knowledge of Japanese art. Open to the public as a museum, Buaiso looks much as it did when the couple lived there, and features Jiro's handmade lighting fixtures and Masako's favorite furnishings throughout. A restaurant and cafe are on the property, as is a garden.

◆46 Iida Family Residence 飯田家住宅 / Yokohama, Kanagawa

The current head of the Iida family in Yokohama City is the seventeenth generation of a line that goes back to a village head in the early Edo period (17th century). The family's yosemune-zukuri thatched-roof minka built in the mid-Meiji period (1868–1912) and its thatched-roof row-house gate built in the late-Edo period sit on five acres and are well maintained. Still used as a private home, neither building is open to the public; but if you are lucky, the gate is sometimes open and you will see what the photo here shows. Both the main house and the row-house gate are important cultural properties, as designated by Kanagawa Prefecture.

㊼ Oginoshima Village 荻ノ島 / Kashiwazaki, Niigata

Oginoshima, located in the heavy snowfall area of the Takayanagi district in Niigata Prefecture, is a rarity in Japan—a ring-shaped village, in which sixty or so traditional farmhouses, about twenty of which have steep thatched roofs (kayabuki), encircle a rice field. For the ultimate experience, visitors can enjoy the region's simple mountain lifestyle if they book a stay at one of Oginoshima's two thatched inns: Ogi no Ie (capacity nine guests) and Shima no Ie (capacity six guests); both are managed by the Oginoshima Furusato Village Association.

OGI NO IE / SHIMA NO IE, OGINOSHIMA KAYABUKI NO YADO
荻の家・島の家
1090-2 Oginoshima, Takayanagi, Kashiwazaki, Niigata

48 Sankyoson 散居村 / Tonami, Toyama

Sankyoson is called a "scattered" village for good reason. The distance between neighboring farmhouses is between 150 and 300 feet, which is extremely rare in a Japanese village. Each house is surrounded by trees, and each house is large, imposing, and well maintained. It is said that people here spend lavishly on their houses, and the attention to detail that goes into every aspect of the village is a pleasure to the eye. There is an observation deck at the top of Mt. Hachibuse. From this designated lookout, 1,400 feet above the ground, you can enjoy a panoramic view of the village and the surrounding rice fields; the view at sunset is especially beautiful.

㊾ Kanazawa 金沢 / Ishikawa

Kanazawa is one of Japan's best preserved feudal cities from the Edo period (1603–1867). Traditional neighborhoods in Kanazawa, include Nagamachi, where residences of mid- and high-ranking samurai sit behind old-fashioned plain earthenware walls that line both sides of narrow, stone-paved alleyways. Fun fact: The earthenware walls are covered with straw mats in winter to protect them from frost. Kanazawa is also known for its three geisha districts, the largest being Higashi Chaya which contains upscale traditional Japanese restaurants (ryotei), teahouses (chaya), and geisha houses. Here, the sounds of shamisen (three-stringed musical instruments) and taiko drums fill the night air.

⑤⓪ Kumagawajuku 熊川宿 / Wakasa, Fukui

The Saba Kaido (Mackerel Highway) connected Wakasa Bay and the port city of Obama—same name, but no link to the former president of the United States—to the inland capital city of Kyoto. Because the imperial court in Kyoto craved the seafood delicacies caught in the bay, carriers either on foot or on horseback were enlisted to quickly transport the perishable cargo of fresh fish, including the precious mackerel which gave the highway its name. The carriers could take a break at several stopovers en route, including the post town of Kumagawa, whose traditional buildings from the Edo period (1603–1867) remain.

⑤① Obama Nishigumi 小浜西組 / Obama, Fukui

Obama, the center of the Wakasa Bay area since ancient times, flourished as a port town on the Sea of Japan coast during the Middle Ages (the Kamakura and Muromachi periods). Later, during the Edo period, it was a seaside castle town, whose castle was mostly destroyed by fire around 1871. Obama's many phases are best experienced in the neighborhood of Obama Nishigumi—an Important Preservation District for Groups of Traditional Buildings—where merchant and samurai houses remain. At the western end of the neighborhood, Sanchomachi, a geisha enclave since the 18th century, adds a further dimension to the town's old-world atmosphere.

52 Oshino Village 忍野村 / Minamitsuru, Yamanashi

The village of Oshino in the eastern section of the Fuji Five Lakes Region has an enviable location at the base of Mt. Fuji, a volcano and Japan's tallest (and unquestionably most famous) peak. The region is picture-perfect all year round. Photographers will want to capture the traditional thatched-roof buildings of Oshino Hakkai, the part of the village whose eight ponds are fed by melting snow from Mt. Fuji. A word of warning: Because Oshino Hakkai has been developed as a tourist site and is included in the Mt. Fuji UNESCO World Cultural Heritage site, it can be as crowded as a theme park, especially on holidays.

53 Aoni 青鬼 / Hakuba, Nagano

Aoni is a small mountain village located northeast of Hakuba in the Japanese Alps. The village owes its distinction as a Preservation District for Groups of Traditional Buildings to its dozen or so large kominka and handful of warehouses built during the Edo (1603–1867) and Meiji (1868–1912) periods. Rice terraces and stone Buddhas enhance the quiet, traditional rural landscape, while the view of the Northern Alps seen beyond the village and fields is breathtaking. The area, which gained international fame when it hosted the Nagano 1998 Olympic Winter Games, remains a prime destination for skiing, snowboarding, and other winter sports.

54 Obuse 小布施 / Kamitakai, Nagano

Katsushika Hokusai (1760–1849), probably Japan's most famous artist, spent the last years of his life in Obuse. Because of Hokusai and the universal popularity of his works, which include the extraordinary series of woodblock prints, *Thirty-six Views of Mt. Fuji*, the once depopulated small country town has been revived. Art lovers flock to Obuse to visit the Hokusai Museum, which opened in 1976, and walk along the beautifully landscaped streets that still retain traces of the Edo period (1603–1867).

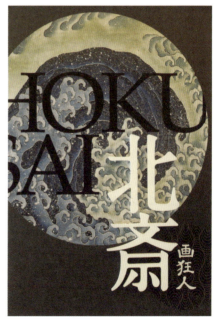

HOKUSAI MUSEUM
北斎館
485 Obuse, Kamitakai, Nagano

55 Naraijuku 奈良井宿 / Shiojiri, Nagano

Imagine it is the Edo period (1603–1867), and you are traveling from Kyoto to Edo (today's Tokyo) on the Nakasendo highway. When you arrive at Naraijuku, a wealthy post town in the mountainous Kiso Valley, you will know that your journey is half over because the town is the thirty-fourth of the sixty-nine post towns (aka stations) on the highway. It is time to rest and relax in a ryokan in Nakamachi, the town center. Just like in the old days, Nakamachi is an enjoyable place in which to stroll, dine, and shop for souvenirs, especially locally made lacquerware. As you amble along the long main street, you will no doubt notice an unusual architectural detail: Traditional kominka have overhanging eaves that are unique to this town.

56 Koshinzuka こうしんづか / Kiso, Nagano

Koshinzuka is a minshuku: a family-operated, Japanese-style bed and breakfast. Built in 1903 (Meiji 36), the rural (somewhat remote) inn is small—there are only three guest rooms—but that's what makes it all the more cozy. The irori (traditional sunken hearth) is popular among guests, who gather around it to talk and dine on locally grown vegetables, river-caught fish, and other seasonal ingredients. According to the current owner, seventy percent of recent guests have been Westerners, with the largest number coming from the United Kingdom. Upon departure, be sure to leave a review of your stay in the minshuku's notebook, which is filled with favorable impressions written in languages from all over the world.

---

57 Mugeiso 無藝荘 / Tateshina, Nagano

The thatched-roof kominka Mugeiso was the longtime home of Yasujiro Ozu (1903–1963), the renowned film director who wrote many of his screenplays there and whose movie *Tokyo Story* (1953) is unanimously acclaimed as his masterpiece. The house is now a museum and memorial to Ozu, who loved the nature, humanity, and delicious sake of Tateshina in Nagano. Sake gave him inspiration, he claimed. The story goes that when he and his writing partner, Kogo Noda, began a new script, they would line up bottles of their favorite sake. As work progressed, bottles emptied. To mark the completion of the script for *Tokyo Story*, Noda wrote in his diary, "Finished, 103 days; 43 bottles of sake."

58 Kasenan Seni Onsen Iwanoyu 花仙庵 仙仁温泉 岩の湯 / Nagano

Kasenan Seni Onsen Iwanoyu is a luxurious hot spring ryokan set in acres of quiet and peaceful woodland. A reservation for a room here is among the most sought-after and therefore the most difficult to get in all Japan. So don't just turn up at the door expecting to be accommodated. I do not exaggerate when I advise you to make a reservation a year in advance. Do that, and you will be amazed by the forest landscape (plenty of walking trails), the Westernized decor of the rooms, the satisfying meals, the hospitality of the staff, and the quality of the hot spring baths (a long soak in the cave bath is an adventure). Experiencing the ambience of a Japanese private home like this is not cheap. Expect the bill at the end of your stay to be high.

59 Gero Onsen Yunoshimakan 下呂温泉 湯之島館 / Gifu

For more than a thousand years, Gero Onsen has been ranked as one of the three best hot springs in Japan; the other two are Arima Onsen in Hyogo Prefecture and Kusatsu Onsen in Gunma Prefecture. Yunoshimakan, an old-time inn quietly nestled on a forty-acre site in the Hida Forest with a commanding view of the town of Gero Onsen below, was founded in 1931 during the early Showa period (1926–1989). The imposing main building, constructed in wood in the sukiya style defined by a stately elegance and grace in harmony with nature, is registered as a Tangible Cultural Property of Japan. Rarely, if ever, are guests permitted to stay in a cultural property, but Yunoshimakan is the exception.

60 Mino 美濃 / Gifu

Mino owed its prominence during the Edo period (1603–1867) to its location on a major highway and its nearness to the Nagara River, a source of cold, clear water that was vital to the town's main industry: the production of traditional handmade washi paper. The style of washi known as Mino washi, which is produced and sold in the town to this day, is characterized by its pure white color, thinness, and durability. Wealthy washi merchants lived in the Udatsu Wall Historical District, named for the decorative yet practical earthen firewalls between houses. As you walk around this Important Preservation District for Groups of Traditional Buildings, study the mushiko windows on the kominka and kura; these latticed windows with fine vertical bars suggest an insect cage.

61 Numazu Club 沼津倶楽部 / Senbonmatsu, Shizuoka

The luxuriously secluded inn is located on two and a half acres surrounded by a pine grove that has survived for centuries. The inn is an exquisite balance of old and new. Both the row-house gate at the entrance and the Meiji-period teahouse, which was built in the sukiya style in 1913 and restored as a restaurant in 2006, have been recognized as Tangible Cultural Properties. A separate villa-like lodge was built in 2006 using natural materials and containing only eight guest rooms, a true indulgence for such a spacious and architecturally novel site. Numazu Club is a hidden gem that not many people know about. I recommend it.

62 Izu Matsuzaki 伊豆 松崎 / Shizuoka

Matsuzaki has been a prosperous port town on the beautiful southwestern coast of the Izu Peninsula since ancient times. There are many sites in the town, but the namako kabe (sea cucumber walls) of Matsuzaki's traditional houses are particularly impressive. Square charcoal-gray tiles cover the exterior walls, while thick white plaster strips—said to resemble sea cucumbers, marine invertebrates that look like the vegetable—overlay and seal the spaces between the tiles. The eye-catching result is an overall diamond pattern. Sea cucumber walls, which are fireproof, moisture-proof, and waterproof, were once seen throughout Japan, but they are now few and far between.

63 Kakujoro 角上楼 / Tahara, Aichi

In the early Showa period (1926–1989), the port town of Tahara facing Mikawa Bay on the picturesque Atsumi Peninsula in Aichi Prefecture boasted a large and very lively hanamachi district, where geisha lived and entertained. In 1929, a traditional wooden building in that district was converted into an inn named Kakujoro. Two modern buildings have been added to the ryokan since then, but it is the original building's interior that retains the retro and peaceful atmosphere of a Showa-era hanamachi. Meals at Kakujoro are prepared with market-fresh fish from the bay, flavorful Atsumi beef, and locally grown produce.

64 Arimatsu 有松 / Nagoya, Aichi

Many Westerners associate tie-dye with the rebellious, counterculture, and free-spirited 1960s and 1970s when hippies wore colorful, boldly patterned tie-dye T-shirts to protest the Vietnam War. Tie-dye represented the alternative to war: peace and love. Tie-dye was also something you could do at home, in your kitchen. Tie-dye amateurs may be surprised when they visit Arimatsu, where artisans in the Edo period (1603–1867) elevated the ancient and traditional handicraft of tie-dyeing cloth for kimono to an art form that is still practiced and revered as Arimatsu Narumi Shibori. Arimatsu's old town features the mansions and machiya (traditional townhouses) of tie-dye owners and workers, as well as shops selling the esteemed textiles.

65 Asuke 足助 / Toyota, Aichi

Once an important relay station for the transportation of salt from Mikawa Bay and products from the Shinshu mountains, Asuke declined when oxen and horses were replaced by more modern and faster means of transportation. Nonetheless, the atmospheric old town has survived, with its traditional Sanshu roof tiles—since the Edo period, Sanshu in Aichi Prefecture has been recognized as one of the three most significant production areas of Japanese tiles—and exterior walls coated in white plaster as a fire prevention measure. Sanshu Asuke Yashiki, an open-air museum of restored kominka from the Meiji period (1868–1912), recreates the life of a mountain village where craftsmen demonstrate weaving and make paper umbrellas.

66 Shiratama 志ら玉 / Nagoya, Aichi

Located just a short distance from central Nagoya, this ryotei (upscale restaurant) is in a charming building made up of a 300-year-old farmhouse, a late-Edo period merchant's house, and a teahouse that have been relocated and restored to their original state. Enchantment begins when you pass through the entrance and a zelkova-tree gate that is over thirty feet long greets you. The restaurant's impeccable kaiseki meals, served in ten private rooms, are composed of carefully selected ingredients, such as fresh seafood and local vegetables, and subtly incorporate seasonal touches. The history and culture of the setting and the impeccable food and service contribute equally to a quietly enjoyable experience.

67 Sakamoto 坂本 / Otsu, Shiga

For centuries, Sakamoto has been the gateway to the temple of Enryakuji, the main temple of the Tendai sect of Japanese Buddhism and a UNESCO World Heritage Site. Getting to the temple complex, founded in 788 atop Mt. Hiei, is easier today than it was in the early Edo period (1603–1897) when the temple was rebuilt, having been substantially destroyed in 1571. Japan's longest cable car travels the one and a quarter miles between the town and the temple in approximately eleven minutes. A stroll through Sakamoto with its inns, kominka (many of which housed monks), and historically important Hiyoshi Taisha Shrine is both peaceful and quiet. In 1997, Sakamoto was selected as a Preservation District for Groups of Traditional Buildings.

68 Omihachiman 近江八幡 / Shiga

Omihachiman, a castle town built in the late-16th century during the Warring States period, became a rural commercial city in the Early Modern (Edo) period. Omi merchants were successful, rich, and seen all over Japan carrying heavy packs suspended from poles balanced on their shoulders; they regularly supplied communities, large and small, with jute and other goods. Omihachiman's well-preserved merchant quarter has been designated as an Important Preservation District for Groups of Traditional Buildings, while the castle's moat is now a picturesque canal often used as a location for period dramas. A boat ride on the canal is a fun way for visitors to soak up the town's atmosphere.

(69) Hotel Koo Otsu Hyakucho ホテル講 大津百町 / Shiga

Up until about fifty years ago, a "koo" was a traditional mutual aid organization. It was in this spirit of cooperation that Hotel Koo Otsu Hyakucho was created. Instead of constructing brand-new hotels in which visitors could lodge, seven 100-year-old machiya townhouses (one townhouse may even be older) in two shopping arcades in Otsu City on the Old Tokaido Highway were completely renovated into comfortable overnight accommodations, thereby helping to preserve and promote the area's culture and customs. The intention was to revitalize the quiet community by attracting tourists who, as they experience Old Japan, also patronize shops and restaurants and, in so doing, fuel the local economy.

70 Gion Shinbashi 祇園新橋 / Kyoto

When in Kyoto, savvy travelers do as the residents do and call a geisha by her local name—geiko—especially in Gion, Japan's largest hanamachi (geisha/geiko district). Gion has been an integral part of Kyoto's cultural history for 340 years since the Edo period (1603–1867). In the traditional entertainment district, which has long served as the gateway to the Yasaka Shrine, there are scores of tile-roofed teahouses. Shinbashi Dori is a particularly pretty cobblestone-paved street lined with wooden machiya (townhouses). You only have to compare the delicate glimmer of paper lanterns along Shinbashi Dori to the blinding neon lights of Tokyo's Shinjuku to know that you are in an Important Preservation District for Groups of Traditional Buildings.

71 Sagatoriimoto 嵯峨鳥居本 / Kyoto

Sagano in the western part of Kyoto has long been renowned for its scenic beauty and refined culture. Readers of *The Tale of Genji* will recognize it as one of the locales in the classic 11th-century novel. A popular destination for sightseers today, the area attracts crowds of visitors. However, Sagatoriimoto within the district is comparatively tranquil. Once a burial ground for Kyoto residents, it has evolved into the temple town of the Atago Shrine. The distinctive feature of this semirural townscape, an Important Preservation District for Groups of Historic Buildings, is the coexistence of traditional Kyoto machiya (townhouses) from the Meiji period and thatched-roof farmhouses.

72 Ishibekoji 石塀小路 / Higashiyama, Kyoto

Ishibekoji is a lane so narrow and so short that it can be overlooked as you walk through Kyoto's historic Higashiyama district. But it is not to be missed; so, be sure to ask for directions. Once you enter the alley, with its beautiful stone pavement, stone walls, and rows of traditional wooden townhouses, you will feel an indescribable Kyoto atmosphere and a strange sensation as if you have slipped back in time. There are several B&B-style inns along the alley, including Ryokan Uemura founded by a former geisha (or as they say in Kyoto, a geiko). If you stay here, you may be lucky enough to experience the Edo-period street tradition of strolling musicians dressed in kimono.

73 Tawaraya 俵屋 / Kyoto

This 300-year-old ryokan in Kyoto may be the world's most famous Japanese inn. Illustrious foreign guests who have stayed here include Leonard Bernstein, Jean-Paul Sartre, Alfred Hitchcock, Tom Cruise, and many others. The inn's owner, who possesses admirable values and aesthetics, and the Kyoto craftspeople (carpenters and other artisans), who support him, have created a delicate and remarkable series of traditional rooms, each with a poetic name and individual decor. Although Tawaraya is grounded in the elegant sukiya style and does not easily fall into the category of minka (old private house), I dare to mention it as one of the ultimate minka in Japan. The inn, untouched by current trends, does not have a website; and it is expensive.

74 Mo-an 茂庵 / Yoshidayama, Kyoto

Mo-an is a lovely cafe deep in the woods at the top of Yoshida, a small mountain in the northeast of Kyoto. The coffee served here is exceptional, and so is the view as you look down on the city of Kyoto. The traditional wooden building dates from around 1912 at the beginning of the Taisho period (1912–1926) and was originally used for tea ceremonies. It is special in that it incorporates the architectural styles of temples and shrines. Since Mo-an is inaccessible by car, be prepared to reach it on foot. But the hike is worth it. The slope, which leads from Philosopher's Path to Mo-an, is lined with old private houses and is one of my favorite walking trails in Kyoto.

75 Kamishichiken 上七軒 / Kamigyo, Kyoto

Of the five geiko (geisha) districts in Kyoto, the oldest is Kamishichiken, located near the thousand-year-old Kitano Tenmangu Shrine in the northwest part of the city. It is also the least well-known of the five hanamachi, being small and off the beaten path. But for a visitor in search of an adventure away from crowds of tourists, that is a plus. Even if it is drizzling, an evening stroll along Kamishichiken's quiet stone streets, with their wooden chaya (teahouses) and okiya (geiko houses), has much to offer, including the sight of geiko and maiko (apprentice geiko) on their way to work as entertainers well-versed in traditional Japanese music and dance.

76 Hirakatashuku 枚方宿 / Osaka

Hirakatashuku was an important and prosperous transportation hub and post town during the Edo period (1603–1867). As the third station on the Osaka Kaido (highway) which joined the cities of Kyoto and Osaka, it was in effect the fifty-sixth of the fifty-seven stations on the famed Tokaido Road, known as the Eastern Sea Route that ran between Edo (present-day Tokyo) and Kyoto, the then-capital of Japan. Hirakatashuku was also a relay port for transportation on the Yodo River. A walk along the old highway for about a mile and a quarter from Hirakata Station will give you a glimpse of the prosperous town of that time, immortalized by Hiroshige in his ukiyoe print, *Kawachi Province, Mount Otoko in Hirakata* (1853).

77 Takenaka Carpentry Tools Museum 竹中大工道具館 / Kobe, Hyogo

The hand tools that master carpenters, plasterers, and other craftsmen have used since ancient times to construct traditional Japanese buildings, like the wooden kominka, temples, and shrines featured in this book, are an indispensable part of Japan's cultural heritage and therefore must be conserved. To this end, Japan's only museum of carpentry tools from the past has a wide-ranging collection of more than 35,000 pieces, including a vast array of chisels, planes, and saws. The artful way in which the tools are displayed, the building, the site, and the overall ambience will appeal to those who love kominka and Old Japan. In addition to its permanent collection, the museum offers lectures and workshops for all ages.

78 Tatsuno 龍野 / Hyogo

Tatsuno is a quiet, moderately sized castle town. Its 1599 fortress atop Mt. Keiro lies in ruins, but another castle dating from 1672 is at the foot of the mountain. Many samurai residences and old storehouses with white earthen walls remain on the town's narrow streets. Tatsuno's main claim to fame today is as a producer of shoyu (soy sauce) that is light in color and delicate to the taste. In a brick building that was once a factory, the Usukuchi Tatsuno Soy Sauce Museum is the world's first museum devoted to soy sauce. Exhibits include brewing tools and other implements that relate to the manufacturing of soy sauce from the Edo period to just before World War II.

79 Izushi 出石 / Hyogo

Izushi, affectionately known as "Little Kyoto" in the Tajima region of northern Hyogo Prefecture, is a beautiful town with a 400-year history that retains to this day the appearance of a traditional castle town. Small enough to explore on foot, Izushi is filled with architectural and historical sites, including the castle ruins; the imposing Shinkoro Clock Tower, built in 1881; and Eirakukan, the oldest kabuki theater in the Kansai region. Izushi is prized for its pure white porcelain, and there are studios in town where you can try your hand at painting the pottery. Izushi soba (buckwheat noodles) and Tajima beef are local culinary delicacies.

80 Gose 御所 / Nara

Gose came into being about 400 years ago during the early Edo period (1603–1867). The Katsuragi River, which runs through the center of Gose, divides the small provincial city in two. The commercial enclave of Nishi Gose, with its merchant houses and storehouses, is on the west (nishi) bank of the river; the temple district of Higashi Gose is on the east (higashi) bank. Gose's configuration has been so well preserved through the years that an illustrated map from the Edo period can still be used to navigate the city today. Many traditional private houses maintain much of their original appearance, giving the area a charming atmosphere.

81 Ouda 大宇陀 / Uda, Nara

The townscape of Uda–Matsuyama in Ouda City, with its beautiful rows of houses with latticework facades built during the late-Edo (1603–1867) and early Showa (1926–1989) periods, is an Important Preservation District for Groups of Historic Buildings. A bird's-eye view of the old town can be enjoyed from the Morino Medicinal Herb Garden, which sits on a hill to the north. The garden, which opened in 1729, is one of Japan's oldest medicinal herb gardens (some say it is the oldest). Among the thatched-roof buildings still in existence in the surrounding area, the Kataoka Residence, the home of a former village headman, is an important cultural property.

82 Ryujin Onsen Kamigoten 龍神温泉 上御殿 / Wakayama

Ryujin Onsen is located almost in the center of the Kii Peninsula on the island of Honshu, deep in the mountains on the border between Wakayama and Nara prefectures. In this small hot spring village, a lodging house was built in the mid-17th century (Edo period) for Yorinobu Tokugawa, the first daimyo (feudal lord) of the Kishu domain. There, he relaxed and bathed in the restorative water. The house is now a ryokan called Kamigoten. If you are lucky, you may be able to reserve the Onarino-ma room where everything, including the furniture, is as it was when Yorinobu Tokugawa stayed there. This is your chance to live like a lord, even if it is only for one night.

83 Kurayoshi 倉吉 / Tottori

Hot spring resorts and lush greenery surround Kurayoshi, located in the center of Tottori Prefecture. Walking slowly through the town's well-preserved merchant quarter, Utsubukitamagawa, one is struck by the pleasant air and a sense of tranquil nostalgia emanating from its storehouses and rows of old merchant houses. White plastered walls, black cedar boards, reddish-brown roof tiles, and small, gently warped stone bridges crossing the Tamagawa river and canal take you back in time to the Edo (1603–1867) and Meiji (1868–1912) periods. In 1998, Utsubukitamagawa was added to Japan's list of Important Preservation Districts for Groups of Traditional Buildings.

84 Misasa Onsen 三朝温泉 / Tottori

Misasa Onsen, a retro hot spring resort not far from Kurayoshi City in Tottori Prefecture, retains the atmosphere of the Taisho (1912–1926) and early Showa (1925–1989) periods. Small inns, restaurants, antiques shops, and souvenir stores line its stone-paved main street. Of special interest is Kajikawa's Barbershop and Museum, which has offered haircuts and shaves for more than 100 years; inside is a fascinating world of tonsorial antiques and memorabilia. If you are staying over, I recommend Ryokan Ohashi, established in 1932 (Showa 7). Built in the traditional wooden style along a stretch of the Mitoku River, the nationally registered tangible cultural property is a spectacular sight when viewed from the opposite bank of the river.

85 Matsue 松江 / Shimane

Once there were thousands of castles in Japan. Of those thousands, only twelve exist today in their original state, having survived wars, natural disasters, and widespread demolition at the end of the feudal age in 1868. Matsue Castle, built in 1611, is one of those survivors. Shiomi Nawate Street, which runs along the imposing castle's moat, is where middle-rank samurai lived. The street's most famous resident, however, was not a samurai, but Lafcadio Hearn (1850–1904), an Irish-Greek writer who fell in love with Japan, changed his name to Koizumi Yakumo, and introduced the West to his adopted country through his many books and essays on Japanese culture and literature. His house and the museum next door are open to the public.

86 Omori Iwami Ginzan 大森石見銀山 / Shimane

Japan was once a major silver producer, and at the beginning of the 17th century, Japanese silver accounted for one-third of the world's total silver production. Iwami Ginzan Silver Mine in Shimane Prefecture, active between 1526 and 1923, was Japan's largest silver mine, and the town of Omori in the valley of the Ginzan River was its administrative and commercial center. Historic 16th-century castle fortresses built to protect the mines, samurai residences, and traditional merchant houses still exist, as do temples, shrines, cemeteries, and stone quarries at the foot of the mountains behind the town. Iwami Ginzan Silver Mine, as well as its cultural landscape, is a UNESCO World Heritage Site.

87 Takahashi 高梁 / Okayama

To distinguish it from other Japanese towns of the same name, the small castle town of Takahashi in Okayama Prefecture is most often referred to as Bitchu–Takahashi. Its most prominent feature is Bitchu–Matsuyama Castle, which sits on a mountain above the town and is the oldest castle still existing in Japan. Dating from around 1240, the castle is also Japan's highest, with an elevation of 1,400 feet. Bitchu–Takahashi's old town streets, with their many restored merchant houses and white-walled samurai residences and gateways, transport visitors back in time to the feudal ages and the Edo period (1603–1867).

88 Tomonoura 鞆の浦 / Hiroshima

The port town of Tomonoura in a bay facing the Seto Inland Sea prospered from trade, both domestically and internationally, during the Edo period (1603–1867). Today, its narrow alleys and lanes look as they did 300 years ago. The port facilities are particularly charming and include the seawall, joyato (lighthouse), gangi (stone stairs between land and sea where boats landed and loaded cargo), tadeba (old dock used for ship repairs), and funabansho (a coastal station that tracked boats coming in and out of harbor). *The Wolverine*, the 2013 movie starring Hugh Jackman, filmed several scenes on location in atmospheric Tomonoura.

89 Onomichi 尾道 / Hiroshima

There are several reasons why many traditional old buildings have survived in the hilly port town of Onomichi. For one, the town was not damaged during World War II. But, more importantly, I believe the values of the local people have a great deal to do with the town's endurance. Quite simply, they cherish old things. Religion may have something to do with it too. For a town as small as Onomichi, there are a great many temples. The mile-and-a-half Temple Walk, which connects twenty-five of them, is a worthwhile way to spend an hour or two. Many movies have been shot in Onomichi, including Yasujiro Ozu's masterpiece, *Tokyo Story*.

Tokyo Story (1953) by Yasujiro Ozu

90 Ryokan Onomichi Nishiyama 旅館 尾道西山 / Onomichi, Hiroshima

Originally a tea garden known as Nishiyama Bekkan, the establishment was reborn in 2023 as Ryokan Onomichi Nishiyama, a luxurious inn composed of six freestanding buildings containing eight guest rooms around a 3,000-square-foot lawn and garden overlooking the Seto Inland Sea. Each building has its own atmosphere and architecture. For example, "Wara" is a traditional Japanese-style house with a wara (rice straw) thatched roof, while "Matsukaze" is a sukiya-style house, meaning it is refined and made of natural materials. The buildings are especially notable and impressive because they date from 1943, a time of conflict when construction materials were in short supply because of World War II.

91 Wakimachi Minamimachi 脇町南町 / Mima, Tokushima

From the Edo period (1603–1867) to the Meiji period (1868-1912), Mima was an important distribution center for Awa indigo dye and cocoon silk. With the decline of the silk industry, the town could have undergone large-scale redevelopment, but fortunately it did not. Instead of being demolished, many traditional buildings have been preserved, especially along the town's main street—Udatsu Old Road, as it is commonly known for the obvious reason. Here, practical, decorative, and costly clay udatsu firewalls separate and protect the wooden homes of rich indigo and silk merchants. Mushiko windows—plaster lattice windows on the low second floors of these old houses—also contribute to Mima's vintage atmosphere.

92 Kasashima Town 笠島 / Honjima Island, Kagawa

For hundreds of years, beginning in the late-16th century, Honjima Island ruled the waves in the Seto Inland Sea. As the most important and powerful of the thirty-odd Shiwaku Islands, the shipping hub was home to the Shiwaku Suigun, a navy revered for the navigational skills of its sailors and the masterful techniques of its shipbuilders. Many of these shipbuilders and carpenters used their craft to build residences in the port town of Kasashima on the northeastern coast of the island. Wooden townhouses from the mid-Edo period to the Meiji period line the streets, earning the town the distinction of being the only Important Preservation District for Groups of Traditional Buildings in Kagawa Prefecture. It is a truly unique port town.

93 Shimayado Mari 島宿真里 / Shodoshima Island, Kagawa

Shimayado Mari is a small and cozy onsen ryokan on the island of Shodoshima in the Seto Inland Sea. The wooden main house dates from the early Showa period (1926–1989) and is a national registered tangible cultural property. Although the current owner has expanded the inn, it has only eight rooms, including one that was renovated from a ninety-year-old warehouse; a ninth room is planned. Beneficial and beautifying hot spring water flows into each room from the source, Satoe Onsen. Shoyu-kaiseki meals feature the rich and abundant locally caught seafood, homegrown vegetables, and Shodoshima soy sauce, which the island has produced for more than 400 years.

94 Yusuhara 梼原 / Takaoka, Kochi

If you go to Yusuhara expecting a traditional town, you are in for a surprise. The spacious streets are not lined with kominka, but with houses that look like they have just been built. Electricity poles and wires are buried underground, a rarity in Japan. And dominating the townscape are six large-scale projects designed by famed modern architect Kengo Kuma, including a hotel, an art gallery, a healthcare facility, and a magnificent library shown here. Yusuhara's natural surroundings inspired Kuma to use Japanese cedar, thatch, and traditional carpentry techniques, thereby earning Yusuhara a place in this book. Yusuhara's buildings are new and eco-friendly, but they feel old and will age well.

95 Yanagawa 柳川 / Fukuoka

Yanagawa started out as a castle town between the Kamakura (1185–1333) and Sengoku (1467–1568) periods, but when fire destroyed the castle in 1872 (Meiji 5), another element of nature—water—became the town's chief claim to fame. Because of its hundreds of miles of canals, Yanagawa is known as "the city of water" and "the Venice of Kyushu Island." One can walk around the preserved old town from the Edo period (1603–1867), but a better option is to cruise the canals in a donkobune (flat-bottom boat) and observe Edo history from the water. The sendosan (boatman) stands in the donkobune's stern, facing the bow, and steers with a long pole. The resemblance to a Venetian gondola ride is unmistakable and just as much fun.

96 Tachibana-tei Ohana 立花邸 御花 / Yanagawa, Fukuoka

Ohana is a luxury hotel—and a microcosm of Japanese history, architecture, and culture. In the 18th century, a traditional Japanese-style wood house on the property was the residence of the Tachibana clan of feudal lords. Japan's feudal era ended in 1868, and the samurai class was abolished shortly thereafter. During the Meiji period (1868–1912), a family member reinvented the estate for the new age, adding the spectacular Shotoen garden and a Western-style building as a guesthouse. An on-site museum exhibits the armor of successive generations of the Tachibana family. Ohana's six acres have been selected as a National Place of Scenic Beauty.

97 Takegawara Onsen 竹瓦温泉 / Beppu, Oita

For centuries, public bathhouses were a staple of everyday Japanese life, giving rise to the bathing culture and ritual known as sento. Around 1970, when bathing facilities in private residences became more commonplace in Japan, the need for public communal bathhouses diminished. Yet the culture persists in certain areas as a means to not only cleanse the body but also connect with the community. Sento is as much a social as it is a hygienic activity, and as such it is popular among foreigners who view it as a vestige of Old Japan that must be experienced. In addition to Takegawara Onsen, founded in 1879 in Beppu, Oita Prefecture, I hope you will also visit the two traditional and old public bathhouses below. They are also architecturally splendid and representative of the periods in which they were built.

DOGO ONSEN HONKAN (BOTCHAN'S HOT SPRING)
道後温泉本館
Built in 1894
Matsuyama, Ehime

KATAKURAKAN
片倉館
Built in 1928
Suwa, Nagano

98 Usuki 臼杵 / Oita

Usuki was a castle town in the 16th century, and even though only fragments of the castle's ramparts survive today, the town itself, especially the Nioza neighborhood, is typical of a castle town from the past with narrow serpentine streets, rows of samurai residences, and temples. Several miles from the center of town is a truly remarkable sight that predates the castle: Usuki's sekibutsu (stone Buddhas). Sixty Buddhas, carved into the solid rock walls of cliffs, are believed to be a thousand years old. These sculptural masterpieces are understandably included on the list of the National Treasures of Japan.

99 Gajoen 雅叙苑 / Kagoshima

As its name implies, Wasurenosato Gajoen is an inn for guests who want to forget (wasure) the hurly-burly of everyday life and find solace and regeneration in a secluded retreat where they can commune with nature. Set in a deep forest next to a river, Wasurenosato Gajoen is like a traditional mountain hamlet (sato). Guest suites are in small thatched-roof traditional houses; meals are made with locally sourced and homegrown ingredients in an open-air kitchen; and the lobby fireplace invites contemplation as effortlessly as it does conversation. Add chickens freely strolling through the garden, and you have the perfect image of Old Japan. Member of Relais & Châteaux, the association of international luxury hotels and restaurants.

100 Izumifumoto 出水麓 / Kagoshima

During the Edo period (1603–1867), Kagoshima's most powerful warrior clan erected as many as 120 outlying castles in various parts of its territory to secure borders and inhibit enemy invasion. Izumi was one of those outer castles. As was the custom, residences for samurai soldiers sprang up around the castle and formed a town; approximately 150 of Izumi's old houses, with trimmed green hedges and stone walls piled up with river stones, still exist and many are even inhabited by descendants of the original samurai. The area is an Important Preservation District for Groups of Traditional Buildings and a reminder of what life was like 400 years ago in feudal Japan.

101 Chiran 知覧 / Kagoshima

Once a castle town militarized for war, Chiran is committed to peace today. Its well-preserved samurai residences from the Edo period (1603–1867) were built to withstand enemy aggression; yet within the fortified gates of these mansion fortresses—in intimate gardens of exquisite invention, beauty, and tranquility—the ambience was and continues to be anything but warlike. Of the samurai gardens open to the public, many are in the minimalist but awesome dry garden style. At the opposite end of town, the Chiran Peace Museum exhibits items relating to World War II's kamikaze pilots, in the hope that a war that produced, in my opinion, the profoundly misguided and tragic kamikaze suicide missions will never happen again.

238　古民家 ♦ *Kominka*

III
MY KOMINKA ODYSSEY AND DIARY

1980s–2007—THE JOURNEY BEGINS

I became fascinated with the traditional Japanese architecture known as kominka in the late 1980s. I was then living in Yokohama City, where I still live today.

I have moved a lot in my lifetime. As a married man, I relocated my family no fewer than ten times. My spouse, Chie, initially accommodated my nomadic tendencies, but when we finally settled into a condominium in 1989, she put her foot down.

"I am done with moving," she said. "If you want to change homes again, you will have to do so without me."

I was taken aback. Chie had established a community in the area through her teachings of koto, sangen, and tea ceremony, and counted many disciples and friends in her network. Relocating would mean losing this community and the connections she had made. In retrospect, I understand why she made such an ultimatum. But at that time I was already engaged in various activities related to the preservation of kominka, and I was increasingly drawn to the idea of living in an old house.

In spite of my wife's reluctance, I eventually brought up the subject. She had a keen eye for traditional architecture, especially when it came to tea ceremony rooms, and, in a way, she knew more about old buildings than I did. I tried to sweet-talk her into the idea by mentioning building a cozy tea ceremony room within the kominka. I also got her involved in the fun events organized by the Japan Minka Revival Association (JMRA), such as koto and sangen concerts, to spark her interest. Through my cunning tactics (I thought they were cunning), I finally persuaded her to agree to consider moving one more time, but only if it was to a kominka.

"Okay, if we can live in an old-fashioned abode, I'll follow you there, but this is our last move," she said with a smirk and an unmistakable air of finality.

At around the same time, our son, Hajime, an art college graduate, was launching his career as a metalcraft artist. He needed a studio in which to work. The gods, it seemed, were with me.

Hence, in 1997, we embarked on a search for a traditional folk house on land near to our condominium in Kanagawa Prefecture that would provide a second home and peaceful country retreat for my wife and me, as well as a studio for Hajime.

Chie playing a koto

Seven Requirements

My son and I, sometimes accompanied by Chie, piled into the car and set out to view properties almost every weekend. This went on for years. Unfortunately, our budget was limited, and there were no suitable properties in Kanagawa. And while I found the search to be a delightful hobby, I now know that it must have been a difficult experience for my family, especially my wife who passed away on January 10, 2005, at the age of fifty-two after battling stomach cancer.

Heartbroken, but knowing that Chie would want me to pursue my dream, Hajime and I continued our search, reluctantly expanding it to neighboring Yamanashi Prefecture. This time, we made a list of what exactly we were looking for:

1. Elevation between 2,000 and 3,000 feet above sea level. The Kofu region in Yamanashi is in a basin and can get hot during the summer, so we decided to look for higher ground to escape the heat. But we didn't want to go too high because that limits the kinds of crops that can be grown, and it was our intention to be as self-sufficient as possible.

2. Southern slope with sunrise and sunset views.

3. Land with forest in the back and unobstructed views in front.

4. A view of city lights. After working for a long time in the busy districts of Ginza and Shinbashi in Tokyo, we missed neon! But even better would be a view of Mt. Fuji.

5. No nearby houses. Not that we intended to be antisocial; rather, we wanted to avoid disturbing neighbors with noise from Hajime's studio.

6. A plot of land between half an acre and an acre.

7. A restorable kominka on the property.

These requirements were demanding, but after more than a decade of looking, we felt that we couldn't compromise any further. Some may call it stubbornness, but we like to think of it as pride.

As my diary reveals, our determination eventually paid off.

2008–2009—FINDING PERFECTION
At last, a promising piece of land!
July 11, 2008. Sunny

Mr. Masao Nozawa, a master builder I met through the Japan Minka Revival Association, phoned today to tell me about a property in Makigaoka Town, Yamanashi Prefecture, that meets almost all seven of my requirements.

Excited, I immediately set off to see the land. Despite its unprepossessing appearance—it looks like a building yard and dumping ground—the location is perfect. And it is just a two-hour drive from our home in Yokohama.

By a stroke of luck, I was able to secure the property with a provisional contract and cancel the advertisement before the listing went public. It has been a long journey to find the perfect piece of land, but after all those years, success!

Looking back, I know I couldn't have found this gem without having clearly defined my conditions. I also needed to seize the opportunity and act decisively on the day Mr. Nozawa called, which I did. I'm thrilled to start a new chapter.

My Kominka Odyssey and Diary 247

Opposite page: The property when first seen. *This page, top,* a view from the property; *bottom,* the village of Somaguchi, Makigaoka

Searching for a Kominka

June 2, 2009

Since no kominka stood on the lot in Makigaoka, I had to find, move, and rebuild one. And so, the search for my dream home began. It would take a year.

My ideal kominka was a house with a grand and traditional feel, solidly built with thick zelkova timbers. Some kominka in the Yamanashi region used zelkova for the main pillar, but most of the other structural timbers were either cedar or pine, and these were thin due to the lack of heavy snowfall in Yamanashi. Consequently, I looked farther afield in the Niigata Joetsu area, a region of heavy snowfall, and the Kyoto, Miyama Town, or Kohoku, Shiga area.

I also browsed the "Minka Bank," operated by the JMRA, that matches owners wanting to sell their kominka with potential buyers.

And I consulted people I had met through kominka activities, such as those in Kyoto and Shiga who dealt with kominka, old timber, and old fixtures. I also approached Karl Bengs, the president of Karl Bengs and Associates in Niigata, with whom I have had a long-standing friendship. I invited Karl to the Makigaoka site and asked him to find a kominka that would fit the land and blend in with the surrounding neighborhood. As the builder of the Bengs House in Matsudai-cho, Niigata, Karl is a specialist in kominka restoration, and I was eager to benefit from his experience and design skills.

The Perfect Old Farmhouse
July 7, 2009

A year after purchasing the land in Yamanashi, Karl and Mr. Shigetaro Ichimura, the president of a local demolition company, arranged for me to see an old Japanese farmhouse in Yasuzuka, Joetsu City, Niigata. Yasuzuka is known for its heavy snowfall. The farmhouse, built in 1911 and located in a forest on a small hill, was a moderate-sized, well-maintained kominka. Its stunning sunken hearth room, made of zelkova wood, which I had long desired, immediately captured my heart. It was love at first sight! Right then and there, I made up my mind. Although finding land had been a challenge, finding the perfect kominka to relocate was relatively straightforward.

I didn't know much about the house, only that a plaque existed confirming that it had been built in 1911 (Meiji 44). After doing some research, I was able to contact the previous owner, Mr. Masataka Kazui, and we talked on the phone. A few days later, Mr. Kazui sent me a gracious letter and a detailed history of the house and his family.

The Kazui family served as village head (shoya) in Ohara Village, Echigo Province (located in Yasuzuka-ku, Joetsu City) from the end

Top, Karl Bengs; *above*, the front of the kominka in Yasuzuka (see **A** on the floor plan on p. 251)

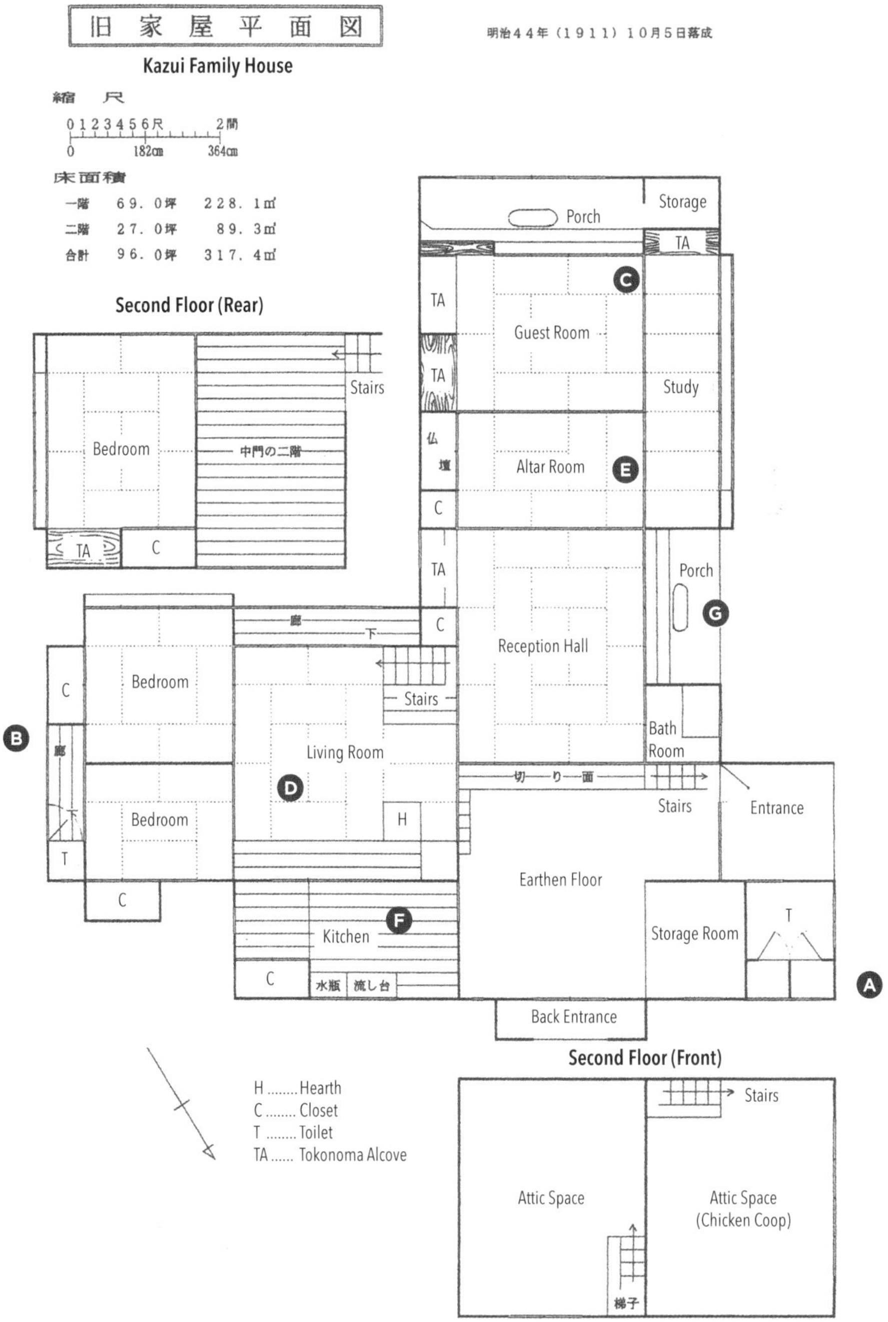

My Kominka Odyssey and Diary 251

旧家屋平面図
Kazui Family House

明治44年（1911）10月5日落成

縮　尺
0 1 2 3 4 5 6 尺　　2間
0　　182cm　　364cm

床面積
一階　69.0坪　228.1㎡
二階　27.0坪　89.3㎡
合計　96.0坪　317.4㎡

Second Floor (Rear)

Bedroom
Stairs
中門の二階
TA
C

Porch
Storage
TA
TA
Guest Room
TA
Study
仏壇
Altar Room
TA
C
Reception Hall
Porch
Bath Room
Stairs
Entrance
Bedroom
C
廊下
Stairs
Living Room
H
Bedroom
C
T
C
Kitchen
水瓶　流し台
切り面
Earthen Floor
Storage Room
T
Back Entrance

A, **B**, **C**, **D**, **E**, **F**, **G**

H .... Hearth
C .... Closet
T .... Toilet
TA ...... Tokonoma Alcove

Second Floor (Front)

Stairs
Attic Space
Attic Space (Chicken Coop)
梯子

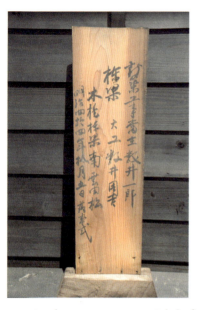

of the Edo period (1603–1867). The family lived in a house built by Mr. Kazui's grandfather, who was the village head at the time. In 1901, a fire in the village destroyed twenty-nine out of forty-two houses, including the Kazui family's house. Only their storehouse survived. Because Mr. Kazui's grandfather was well-versed in construction—in addition to his own house, he had supervised the building of the local elementary school—he rebuilt his home. But it took him ten years to design and acquire the necessary materials before construction could finally begin on April 14, 1910 (Meiji 43). The groundbreaking ceremony was on October 7, 1910 (Meiji 43), followed seven months later by the raising of the main house's frame on May 6 and 7, 1911 (Meiji 44). The completion ceremony was held on October 5, 1911.

I am indebted to Mr. Kazui for this information, and I will always treasure his letter.

"Dear Sir," he wrote. "Thank you for taking over my house. I am deeply grateful to you for doing so. It was with a heart filled with sadness that I thought about the house that my grandfather built with great effort being destroyed without mercy in my generation. However, when I heard that it will be taken over by you and rebuilt in Yamanashi, I was relieved. I am sure that my grandfather and the house will be happy.

"Once again, I deeply express my gratitude. I hope to visit at the time of completion. Regarding the building plaque, I would like to give it to you who will cherish the house. I think it would be most appropriate to keep it in the revived house."

AUTHOR'S NOTE: To this day, the plaque (above) is on display in the gallery room next to the earthen floor.

Developing Architectural Drawings

August 2009

Having found the building, it's time to work on the design. I asked Karl to help. He agreed, and we met.

First, we laid out the site. The land is approximately half an acre. Based on its shape and orientation, we decided where to rebuild the main house. We chose the back of the site which overlooks the Kofu Basin and faces Mt. Fuji. This means the position of the entrance of the original kominka will change significantly. We then decided where to construct my son's studio, and where to create the garden (and what kind of garden it will be). Karl suggested adding a pond. Great idea!

Next, we considered how best to restore the old house. One of the principles of the design is to effectively maintain the strength of the building by using the original wooden frame and structure. However, given the expected use of the house, we plan to make appropriate changes in the layout, etc., but without affecting the basic structure.

After our discussion, Karl came up with the initial architectural design. His plan emphasized creating a roomy open space by lowering the floor of the original one-story house and partially removing the ceiling to create an open ceiling. The roof of the building is to be raised, and its shape changed to provide loft and storage space. Additionally, a large opening is to be made on the southern wall to accommodate the beautiful view of the basin and Mt. Fuji. He also expanded the earthen floor as a future gallery area. Based on Karl's plan, my son and I created various floor plans of our own, incorporating our hopes as well as the various modern conveniences we thought were essential. This collaborative stage was not only enjoyable, it was exhilarating.

The work of developing architectural drawings took about three months. Looking back, I think it would have been better if I had taken more time at this stage and collected more information and considered various options. But as we progressed with the

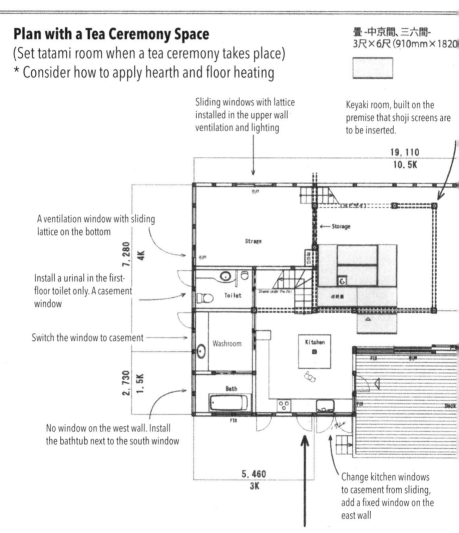

My Kominka Odyssey and Diary 255

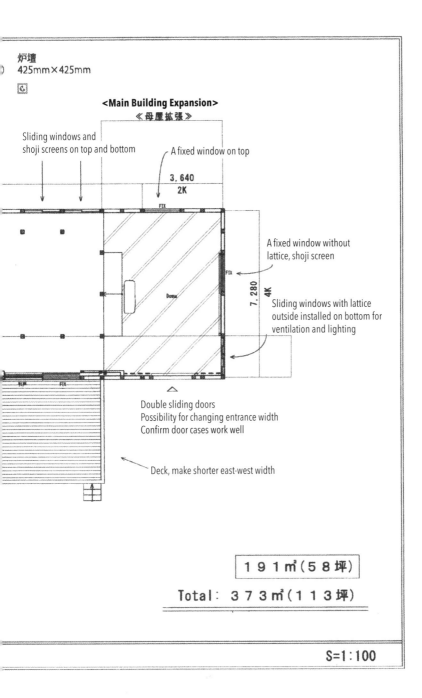

256 古民家 ♦ *Kominka*

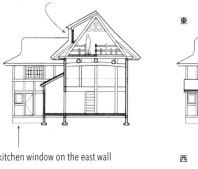

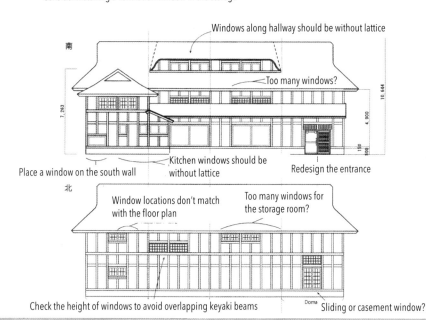

HOUSE OF HASEGAWA   (edited by Hajime)   S=1:100

construction, I gradually realized that restoring a kominka is not like building a new house. Unexpected obstacles can arise due to the old materials used, and new ideas may emerge, leading to changes in the plan. So, we decided to proceed without relying too much on the detailed plans. If we were to enjoy the challenge in a positive way, we had to learn to be flexible, think on our feet, and improvise when necessary.

How Much Will It Cost?

September 2009

With the general plan for the restoration of the kominka taking shape, we knew we had to find a contractor who would enjoy the "challenge" with us. Fortunately, we found such a contractor. We asked Nozawa Jyuken Co., Ltd. to submit a schedule and an estimate for the cost of construction. Mr. Masao Nozawa, who introduced us to the land, manages the company.

    As I have previously said, changes to an initial plan and unforeseen obstacles arise during construction; therefore, it is not possible to account for every detail at this early stage. Rough estimates are acceptable. And that is what Nozawa Jyuken provided, estimating a completion time of ten months and a cost of 36 million yen ($257,000)*. Given Nozawa Jyuken's proven success in restoring kominka, we judged the estimates to be fair, and so we entered into a formal contract. Other costs had already been determined, including the acquisition fee for the kominka, the demolition and transportation costs, and the cost of the architectural drawings. In total, those amounted to approximately 10 million yen ($71,000). We were definitely on our way.

* US $1 = 140 yen (2023)

Moving the Old Timbers to Their New Home
November 26, 2009. Clear

The dismantling of the house took about two weeks from October 29. During the disassembly, valuable fittings and old timbers were carefully numbered and stored in a warehouse so that it would be clear where each piece belonged when the house was reassembled.

Yesterday, these structural materials were loaded onto two ten-ton trucks and departed from Joetsu City for their new home in Yamanashi. The trucks drove through the night, arriving safely at 8 a.m. today in Makioka-cho. A large crane was on-site, ready to unload the old timbers, stones, and fittings as soon as the trucks pulled up. The people transporting and receiving the materials are professionals, so they handled the large amount of old timbers with care and caution.

Shiguchi joinery on the beams

As I watched the unloading, which proceeded smoothly and without incident, I marveled at the magnificence of the beams. I stood in awe of their size and heft, completely captivated by the artistry of the handwrought and nail-free shiguchi joinery created by skilled carpenters a hundred years ago. I could not resist complimenting them on their outstanding work.

The stepping stones to be used for the entrance hall were also brought in. Later on, the fittings were transported by a four-ton truck to a facility where they will be stored until needed.

I should have known everything would go well today: The weather was good, and Mt. Fuji could be seen clearly in the distance.

Groundbreaking Ceremony

December 22, 2009. Winter Solstice

Today, as the end of the year approaches, we held a groundbreaking ceremony to pray for the successful start of construction in the new year. The day, an auspicious day in the old Japanese calendar, was blessed with clear weather and an unexpected warmth for this time of year. In the crystalline air, Mt. Fuji, crowned with snow, loomed large and seemed to be celebrating and praying with us for the success and safety of our project. Above all, I want us to enjoy building our house.

My son, Hajime, turns the first sod at the groundbreaking ceremony

2010—REBUILDING THE KOMINKA
My Goals and How I Will Achieve Them

As construction approached, I clarified in my mind what exactly I hoped to achieve in reconstructing this kominka.

Because I wanted a living space with a nostalgic air and a soothing atmosphere that had been created over time, I would use old wood and antique fixtures, as well as natural materials (solid wood, paper, plaster, diatomaceous earth, and wool for insulation). While I would insist on authentic materials, I would avoid expensive ones. I wanted a beautiful space, undivided into small rooms and with its pillars and beams exposed. I wanted a house that was considerate of physical and mental health, environmentally friendly, and adapted to the local climate and customs. I would seek out domestic and locally sourced wood such as hinoki (Japanese cypress), kuri (Japanese chestnut), sugi (Japanese cedar), and kiri (Paulownia). There would be no fake new building materials, such as plywood, laminated lumber, and petroleum-based vinyl wallpaper. That said, I also wanted the house to be modern and comfortable, with heated floors and a functional kitchen. Finally, I would make the most of the view of Mt. Fuji by day and moonlit skies by night, and I would plant simple gardens that would not obstruct the view.

We celebrate the beginning of construction. *From left,* Karl Bengs, Kazuo Hasegawa, Hajime Hasegawa, and master builder Masao Nozawa

Ground Leveling

January 26, 2010. A clear day with auspicious energy

Finally, construction began today. First, the roller work to level the ground. Pressure-resistant reinforcement for the foundation was also started. The foundation is one of the most important elements in building a house. To be extra cautious, the Swedish weight sounding (SWS) test was conducted on December 16 last year to evaluate the soil, its strength, and suitability for construction. Fortunately, no problems were discovered, and so construction was given the go-ahead.

Laying the Foundation

February 10, 2010. Cloudy, with rain later

The foundation work, begun on January 26, was completed today with the installation of reinforced concrete footing on top of the pressure-resistant and crushed stone layer. Next up is the construction of the rising foundation with reinforced concrete. At the same time as the foundation work, the timber for the base plate is being processed. Japanese chestnut, which is resistant to water damage, is being used for the base plate. Recently, it has become quite difficult to obtain high-quality chestnut timber, but we were able to procure it with the help of Mr. Nozawa, the master builder.

The chestnut timber for the base plate is processed while the concrete foundation sets

Raising the Keyaki Pillars

February 25, 2010. Sunny

Today, the first strong wind of spring blew in Yokohama. But in Yamanashi, you can still enjoy the beautiful snowscape of Mt. Fuji!

The chestnut timber for the base is fixed. While new homes often use plastic resin "neko-ishi" footers between concrete foundations and bases, this house is being constructed with durable granite "neko-ishi" footers, assuming a century-long residency.

The old timbers have been repaired, and new joints have been made. Finally, the assembly of the old materials for the structure begins. First, the keyaki (zelkova) pillars and beam for the central part of the house are lifted and secured by a crane. They are heavy, with the combined weight of these two pillars and one beam being in excess of 1,300 pounds. The keyaki timber is splendid. I wonder how many years have passed since the keyaki first started to grow. It probably took at least 200 to 300 years before such timber was ready to harvest.

A crane lifts the first of the old timbers into place

The walls around the building are fixed to the concrete foundation, but the center is constructed using the traditional Japanese method by which the keyaki pillars are neither fixed to the foundation nor deeply rooted in the ground but stand unattached on granite cornerstones called ishibadate. The ishibadate technique reduces shaking caused by earthquakes and is also suitable for Japan's hot and humid climate. It can be said that this project aims to use the best traditional and modern construction methods.

Clockwise from top left: Making a shiguchi joint; granite "neko-ishi" footers; repairing old timbers; assembling a beam; Karl Bengs and Mr. Nozawa; a keyaki pillar stands unattached on a granite cornerstone

Framing the First Floor

March 11, 2010. Clear

The weather has been bad for the past few days, delaying construction. Yesterday, cold weather gripped the nation, and spring snow fell in various places, including Yamanashi where we are. But today it is sunny, and the frame of the first floor is almost complete.

A view of Enzan city in the distance

Working in a Springtime Paradise

April 6, 2010. Clear

The peach trees have begun to bloom at the same time as the cherry blossoms are in full bloom. Beautiful pink colors decorate the Koshu Road. It's like Shangri-La.

Amid the spring blossoms, work on rebuilding the kominka has moved on to the roof. The design has been changed from the original gable roof to a hip roof. New materials are being used to construct it. First, a ridge beam has been made out of cedar wood. Careful measurements are taken to ensure that the roof has the same 45-degree slope as the traditional houses in the Enzan district of Yamanashi.

Constructing the kominka's hip roof

Suwa Taisha Onbashira Festival

April 11, 2010. Rain, occasional sun later

Today, I took the day off to do something I've always wanted to do. I went to the Onbashira Festival. The festival is the biggest and most important ritual of Suwa Taisha, a grand shrine complex around Lake Suwa in Nagano Prefecture. The festival is only held every seven years and involves rebuilding the sanctuaries and erecting large, 200-year-old fir trees called onbashira—"honorable pillars"—at the four corners of the shrine. Among the rituals, the Kiotoshi (tree falling), where sixteen onbashira logs slide down a steep hill from the mountains to the village, is famous for its impressive and heroic nature. I felt it would be auspicious for me to make every effort to attend the festival this year because of the restoration.

Hundreds of parishioners chant and tug on thick ropes as they bring the trunk of a giant fir tree to the steep slope

When it was time for the Kiotoshi to begin, the gods smiled, and the rain stopped. The sacred pillar is over sixty-five feet long, has a diameter of three feet, and weighs over ten tons. Hundreds of parishioners chant and tug on thick ropes as they bring it to the steep slope, where purification salt is scattered. A loud roar echoes throughout the venue. A trumpet sounds, and a red flag is lowered. Spectators hold their breath. An eerie tension fills the air. The massive pillar slowly starts to move, picks up speed, and rushes down the 35-degree slope. About ten people ride on top, but due to the speed, some are thrown off. Others somersault in the air. It is truly a life-threatening event, but there were no serious casualties. After about a hundred yards, the tree stopped amid much jubilation. Success!

Before I left, I visited one of the four shrines to pray for our kominka.

Some parishioners ride–and fall off–the "sacred pillar" as it descends the hill

The Ridge Beam
April 12, 2010. Rain

The ridge beam has been installed, and the house is finally taking shape.

Topping-out Ceremony
April 19, 2010. Sunny

On this beautiful spring day with clear skies, we reached an important milestone: the completion of the basic structure (including pillars, beams, and the roof ridge) and the installation of the ridgepole. We held a topping-out ceremony. Although it is called a ceremony, there was no formal ritual. We simply poured locally produced Koshu white wine on the structural frame of the roof, and prayed for the safe completion of the renovation and for the longevity of this house.

    Afterward, we enjoyed a barbecue in the warm sunshine with the six crew members, raising a toast with the Koshu wine which pairs well with barbecue. Drinking wine with the best staff in the best mood was a pleasant and invigorating experience. Although there have been many rainy days and some minor delays, we are not rushing the work and the project is progressing smoothly in every way.

Mt. Fuji showed its face today, as if to celebrate the completion of the framework with us.

Clockwise from top: The basic structure is now complete; the occasion calls for delicious barbecue; the staff celebrates with a commemorative photo; pouring Koshu wine on the roof's timber frame

As the Local Fruit Grows, So Does the House

May 28, 2010. Clear

To reach the construction site, you need to take the Chuo Expressway and get off at the Katsunuma IC, then drive along the Fruit Line toward the Makigaoka area. As the name suggests, the road passes through a lush orchard. The season of cherry blossoms and peonies has passed, and now fresh green leaves grow thick, and fruits are ripening. Due to the prolonged period of unstable weather this year, the harvest is expected to be one to two weeks later than usual, but the prime cherry season—this region's cherries have a delicious, sweet taste—will begin in early June.

The best quality grapes in Japan are also starting to ripen. The couple who own the orchard nurture each and every bunch of grapes by hand. From summer to autumn, their grapes will grow into the largest Kyoho grapes in the country.

We're ready to install the roof!

The Kyoho vineyard near the construction site

My Kominka Odyssey and Diary 273

Work inside the house advances at a steady pace

Opposite page: The wood framework of the kominka's interior is intricate and meticulously assembled. *This page:* Master carpenters craft the interior with hand tools; massive green tarps enclose the structure and ensure that work can continue uninterrupted, rain or shine

Up on the Roof in Summer
July 8, 2010. Clear

It's the middle of the rainy season, but the sun is shining today. It's a real summer day. In the peach orchard that delighted us in the spring, we can now see an abundance of peaches ready to be harvested. The grape clusters have also grown quite large, and each bunch is being covered with a paper bag to protect the fruit from pesticides. This is truly meticulous work. I doubt any other country goes to such lengths in their farming techniques.

    The restoration work on the kominka has entered the roofing and wall/flooring phase. We had considered using copper for the roof, but due to the significant rise in copper prices, we had to give up on that idea. Instead, we will use galvanized steel plate shingles. Although galvanized steel is slightly more expensive than regular steel, it is said to last longer, and it is malleable, meaning it can be pressed to make delicate curves in the same way as copper.

    The roofing will be done by Takei Sheet Metal Works, which was founded in 1917. Both the third-generation owner, Hirotake Takei, and the fourth-generation owner, Osamu Takei, have an admirable work ethic. "Please tell us if there is anything you need," Osamu says. "We will do everything we can to accomplish it!" His eagerness and easygoing personality make working with them a

Hirotake and Osamu Takei carefully position galvanized steel plate shingles on the roof

pleasure. As this is a job high off the ground, I remind them to be careful and avoid any accidents.

Flooring Elevated to a Fine Art

July 21, 2010. Sunny

The hottest day of the summer so far.

    Last weekend, I attended the opening party of Bengs House in Matsudai, Niigata. Karl purchased the house, an old inn, to revitalize the town, and he has transformed it into a restaurant and office space. Once again, I was impressed by Karl's wonderful renovation work, and it was an inspiring experience. Afterward, I traveled to various towns and houses, such as Sankyoson in Toyama, Mikuni in Fukui, Nagahama in Shiga, and the old thatched-roofed houses in Kyoto's Miyama-cho. I took photographs everywhere. On my way back, I visited a friend in Ontake, Gifu, before returning to the site in Makigaoka to check up on how my kominka is coming along.

The solid hinoki floor planks are long and wide

The flooring work is in full swing. The material for this project is solid hinoki wood with knots and sinuous grain patterns, rather than straight grain patterns as is often seen in traditional Japanese architecture. This was a deliberate choice. I don't think that a design made up of straight grain patterns, like that in a tea ceremony room, is necessarily beautiful. Rather, knots and cloudlike curves in the grain are much more suitable for our kominka. Of course, this also has the advantage of being more affordable. Also, while the standard width of flooring materials these days is mostly around three inches, we needed wider planks due to the large floor space, so we asked our master builder, Mr. Nozawa, to procure thirteen-foot-long, two-inch-thick, nine-inch-wide hinoki planks. I'm looking forward to seeing the completed space with this flooring in place.

The Importance of Good Insulation

August 9, 2010. Overcast, with light rain

It's been an unusually hot summer in Japan. But in spite of the heat, restoration work is progressing steadily. Ironically, we made some important decisions about insulation today—and how best to keep this old house warm in winter!

Yamanashi's Makigaoka area, where we are, isn't very cold during the winter. The coldest it gets is around twenty-five degrees Fahrenheit. And since it snows only a few times a year, there is hardly any accumulation. But, and it is a big "but," when it comes to living comfortably in a renovated kominka, heating is a very important factor.

Originally, we had planned to use glass wool, which is widely used for its low cost and efficiency, as our insulation material. However, we decided against it. The reason being that inhaling the glass fiber dust in glass wool can cause respiratory illnesses and have negative effects on the eyes and skin. Some people argue that the fibers are thicker than those of asbestos, making it safe to use. But we decided to err on the side of caution and prioritize safety and health above all else.

Also, we had pledged to use natural materials as much as possible. That's why we chose natural wool as our insulation material. In addition, the master carpenter, Mr. Nozawa, made a cost-effective proposal to incorporate insulation made of recycled paper. The ceiling and walls are to be insulated with four-inch-thick natural wool, and the underfloor with four-inch-thick recycled paper. Economical, energy-efficient, and environment-friendly: What's not to like?

Natural wool insulation

The loft on the third floor is coming along. We can't wait to see how the town of Enzan and Mt. Fuji will look from up there.

Solid Wood—and Only Solid Wood for This Kominka
September 10, 2010. Cloudy, then sunny

The most important material in this renovation is solid wood. The old timber in the farmhouse is, of course, solid wood, but we have also decided to use domestically produced solid wood for the new timber—even though manufacturers claim that engineered wood, or particle board, performs just as well as solid wood.

Solid wood, especially wood grown in Japan's natural environment, readily adjusts to Japan's hot and humid climate, making it ideal for long-term use. Wood breathes and is a "living material." Even after the tree is cut down and prepared for use as timber, it can still absorb or release moisture in the air to suit the surrounding temperature and humidity.

Additionally, solid wood has cushioning properties and can absorb impact. Compared to metal, glass, and concrete, it has low thermal conductivity and therefore excellent insulation properties. Moreover, the fragrant scent of Japanese cedar and cypress has a relaxing effect on people. There is no reason not to use such a wonderful material.

But I can't say that I know everything about wood. So, today, I visited the local Fujiwara Lumber Store, which is supplying our timber and insulation materials, and took a "crash course" on-site.

My Kominka Odyssey and Diary 281

Top, left and right, Mr. Fujiwara educates us about solid wood

Fujiwara Lumber Store has been in business for three generations. Its current president, Kazushige Fujiwara, showed me around the spacious lumber yard, and my "education" began with a "tutorial" on wood grains. Can an amateur, like me, tell the kind of wood just by looking at the grain? No, Mr. Fujiwara said, and I had to agree. That's when he explained the different grains clearly. I know more now than I did before.

Out of curiosity, I wanted to know the percentage of solid wood his store ships annually. I expected it to be between thirty and forty percent, but I was wrong. It's only ten percent, he said. I couldn't believe my ears, so I repeated the question. But I had heard correctly. I was still surprised but also pleased that materials for our kominka would be in that ten percent.

Storage Doors and Antique Fittings

September 14, 2010. Sunny, with occasional rain

Left, Asahi Kominka and Antique Fittings Center; *right,* a solid keyaki storage door

Antique fittings are an essential aspect of renovating a kominka. While we will incorporate the fittings from the original house that was moved from Niigata, we are also seeking out fittings from other kominka to add an original touch to the new structure.

To this end, we visited two experts in antique fittings: Mr. Akimitsu Kakehata from Chiba, the representative of Asahi Kominka and Antique Fittings Center; and Mr. Hideki Kobayashi from Shin-Kiba, the representative of Hideshina Trading Company. Both specialize in collecting and selling antique materials, and have been friends working together to preserve kominka for a long time.

Mr. Kakehata's warehouse is full of various types of antiques and old folk tools. His vast array of storage doors, or kura-do, is said to be one of the largest collections of its kind in Japan. Mr. Kobayashi, originally a lumber dealer in Kiba, has an extensive stock of fittings. We ended up selecting two magnificent storage doors made from keyaki (Japanese zelkova) wood from Mr. Kakehata and three antique fittings from Mr. Kobayashi.

Jindai Keyaki: Japan's Rarest Solid Wood
September 21, 2010. Cloudy

Today, we headed to Joetsu City in Niigata in search of keyaki timber for the main beam of the entrance and the kitchen island table. Mr. Ichimura, who introduced and dismantled the kominka we are renovating, told us that he has what we want. Mr. Nozawa, the master carpenter, accompanied us on a four-ton truck.

Mr. Ichimura, who dismantles about a hundred buildings annually, has stockpiled large amounts of old materials in various locations, including a warehouse that was once the gymnasium of an elementary school. One of his stockyards had many keyaki timbers, including a splendid one that was originally the main beam of a kura (storage house). It was exactly what we were looking for, so we bought it.

We also loaded the truck with several more keyaki and cedar timbers that will be used for pillars and an overhead grate above the irori (sunken hearth).

Next, we went to the gym warehouse, which was filled with masses of antiques, architectural fittings, and even old furniture and stone statues. There, we encountered the legendary jindai

Master builder Nozawa *(right)* sees jindai keyaki for the first time

keyaki (carbonized Japanese zelkova) wood, hitherto unknown to me. While jindai sugi (carbonized Japanese cedar) is well known, I was told that jindai keyaki is much more rare and hardly ever seen. Mr. Nozawa was awestruck.

"I had heard that it existed, but this is my first time actually seeing it," the master carpenter said in amazement.

To celebrate the realization of my dream of restoring a kominka, Mr. Ichimura offered to sell me this precious jindai keyaki at an exceptional price. I hesitated, wondering if such a valuable antique material might be too luxurious for my home. But perhaps it was fate that had brought us together. So, with gratitude for the kindness and support of so many people, I decided to accept the offer, and we took the wood back to our workshop with the other timbers.

I am excited to see how the antique materials we collected today will be reborn in our kominka.

Izu Stone: A 20-Million-Year-Old Romance

October 12, 2010. Partly cloudy

When wet, Izu stone *(left)* changes to a vivid light blue-green color *(right)*

In line with our commitment to using natural materials, it was our intention to visit the places where they are sourced and learn about them firsthand. We wanted to choose materials that we could see and touch in person, so we could be sure of their quality.

In particular, we were considering what material to use for the bathtub. Wood and stone were the two main candidates, but we eventually decided on stone. This was partly because I had read in a book that Izu stone, which is found in the Izu region, is perfect for use as a bathtub.

I contacted several stone merchants, but no one carried Izu stone. Although it was widely used as a building material during the Edo period and was once plentiful and highly valued, it seems to have fallen out of use and been supplanted by imported stone. Can it be that domestically sourced stone is facing the same difficulties as domestically sourced wood?

Undeterred, I browsed the internet and finally found a mining company, Tokai Saiseki Kogyo Co., Ltd. located in Izu-Nirayama, which offered to show me around its mining site. A considerable number of companies once mined Izu stone, but now there is only Tokai Saiseki Kogyo Co., Ltd. Excited and curious, I drove to Izu-Nirayama.

The company president, Hidehiko Watanabe, met me at the large open-pit quarry and filled me in on how Izu stone is mined.

Tokai Saiseki Kogyo's open-pit quarry

First, it is cut into blocks; then the blocks are taken to the factory adjacent to the quarry where they are further cut to the size needed for a specific project.

According to Mr. Watanabe, Izu stone is a rock that was formed by the compression of lava and volcanic ash that erupted from an underwater volcano about twenty million years ago and was uplifted from the seafloor due to plate movements. He enthusiastically listed the characteristics of Izu stone. When wet, it changes to a vivid light blue-green color. Perfect for a bathtub, I thought. The surface of the stone has holes for air bubbles, making it less slippery when wet. Beautiful and safe! Also, it is easy to process because it is a soft stone, and it works well with concrete. And finally, it is low-maintenance. I was sold! Izu stone was more than I could have imagined, and so I calculated the amount needed on the spot and had a piece cut for me.

With help, I carefully loaded over 700 pounds of stone into the car, which moved slowly and heavily under the weight. But I didn't care. I was in fantasyland and kept repeating to myself: "Twenty million years old! Imagine soaking in a tub from twenty million years ago! How romantic!" I left the mining site feeling as if I were transporting a precious gemstone.

AUTHOR'S NOTE: Tokai Saiseki Kogyo Co., Ltd. went out of business around 2015, and it is currently difficult to obtain new Izu stone.

Indoor Painting

October 20, 2010

We have started to paint the inside of the house.

One of the policies my family and I laid down when starting this project was to participate in the renovation work ourselves. We wanted this to be a collaboration between us and the professionals we hired. But, in reality, the only work that I—an amateur (and clumsy amateur at that)—can do is paint. And even then, I can't work in high places because it's dangerous. So, my son and I started to paint the columns, beams, and other structural elements within our reach. Thanks to Karl, the paint is made of natural pigments and has been imported from Germany.

It's a beautiful autumn day, and it's the lunch break. A refreshing autumn breeze blows through the house. The chief carpenter, Mr. Kusunoki, is taking a nap.

A Catastrophe Averted
October 28, 2010. Rain

An inward hinged wooden window from Germany

The wooden window frames that were ordered from Germany at the end of July arrived in Yokohama by sea, and, after passing through customs, they finally got here two days ago.

Karl recommended these frames, manufactured by Holzbau Winter GmbH, for their insulation and airtightness. Although aluminum window frames are overwhelmingly used in Japan, they have a high thermal conductivity that is a thousand times greater than wood—in other words, they provide poor insulation. When unpacked, the German-made wooden frames were flawless, both in terms of quality and design, just as we expected.

However, there was a problem. We had ordered two types of windows: sliding windows and outward hinged windows. But inward hinged windows were delivered! Our plan had been to install shoji screens on the inside of the windows, but with inward-opening hinged windows, that would be impossible.

If this were a domestic product, we could resolve the problem immediately. But if we were to reorder from Germany, we would have to halt construction for several months until the new wooden frames arrived. Even if we were to proceed with other work, the project would be significantly disrupted and delayed.

I panicked and contacted Karl.

Mr. Nozawa, Karl, and I quickly gathered to brainstorm. Soon, the master carpenter proposed something outside the box. He suggested making shoji screens that hang like temple doors and move on casters.

Well, that's a good idea! Three heads are better than one, and good can come from misfortune. Problem solved. We were able to create interesting windows with a unique design.

AUTHOR'S NOTE: However, I occasionally bump my head against the temple-style hanging shoji screens, even now many years later as I prepare my kominka diary for publication!

Clockwise from top left: Shoji screens hang like temple doors above the inward hinged windows; shoji screens lowered halfway; shoji screens lowered all the way; an unobstructed view through the windows when the shoji screens are not in use

Creating an Innovative Space
November 8, 2010. Clear

Work has begun on installing the ridge beam, provided by Mr. Ichimura of Joetsu, at the entrance of the living room. This beam was used in the Japanese traditional shoin-zukuri style in the house from which it came, but we have decided to change the style in keeping with the overall concept of our project.

I believe that there are three main approaches to renovating a kominka.

The first focuses on modernizing the plumbing and toilet facilities to make the house more livable, but without altering the building's structure. This method aims to faithfully restore the original layout and form of the traditional house.

The second selects parts of the kominka, such as old pillars, beams, or fittings, and incorporates them into the interior design of a room or a shop, giving it a kominka-style look. While admirable for using and preserving old materials, this approach can be problematic if and when the space is renovated again and the traditional materials are discarded.

The third creates a new space with a clear concept and a fresh perspective while maintaining the basic structure and features of the original building. When renovating, it is important to make changes to the original structure with careful consideration. With a solid concept and the right skills, it is possible to boldly create a space that reflects one's lifestyle and preferences, which is the true charm of revitalizing a kominka.

I am following the third approach. I have maintained the basic structure of the house while relocating the entrance, enlarging the earthen floor, raising the ceiling to create a wide-open space, and changing the roof from a gable roof to a hip roof to accommodate the loft. I have also removed the dais, or raised platform, which is a remnant of the feudal era.

Autumn is fully with us. The rice plants have been harvested in the terraced fields next door to the site and are drying in the sun prior to being threshed. It's a beautiful sight.

My Kominka Odyssey and Diary

Before *(top)* and after *(below):* a traditional space reborn

A Painting Mishap During Korogaki Persimmon Season
November 19, 2010. Sunny

The season for sun-drying the famous Korogaki persimmons of Enzan, Yamanashi, has arrived. These persimmons are large, round, and astringent. But after peeling and drying for three to four weeks, they are transformed into deliciously sweet dried persimmons. The many farms around Erinji, the Buddhist temple of warlord Takeda Shingen, are engaged in drying Korogaki persimmons; they are a local attraction at this time of year.

Painting continues at the construction site. I help when I can because I enjoy observing how the color of the wood changes as it is painted. But I am clumsy! While painting, I tried to turn around on a six-foot-high ladder and ended up falling with the bucket of paint in my hand. Fortunately, I was not injured, but the spilled paint made a mess. I am extremely sorry for the trouble caused. It goes to show that I should not do things I am not used to doing.

Top, persimmons drying at Iwanami Farm; *above,* Amakusa mansion near Enzan Station

Plastering the Exterior Walls
November 25, 2010. Sunny

The time has come to begin plastering the exterior walls. The plaster we are using is a mixture of slaked lime, glue (such as seaweed glue), susa (fibrous materials, like hemp, that prevent cracking), and water. With its high resistance to fire, it has been used in Japan to protect valuable properties, such as storehouses, for ages. This excellent natural material controls moisture, and is therefore suitable for Japan's climate, which changes drastically from season to season.

It is late autumn, and winter is just around the corner. It is generally recommended to avoid plastering in winter since the cold can cause cracking during the drying process. I have great confidence in our plaster, but it is still better to finish before the onset of full-blown winter.

Plastering is arduous work due to the large surface area of our kominka's walls. But our plasterer, Shinobu Ito, who is sixty-seven years old, is a professional with fifty years of experience. He begins the job by applying a layer of mortar.

The Scaffolding Comes Down

December 17, 2010. Cold, but sunny

It's the busy end-of-the-year season, but I feel like time is passing slowly here at the restoration site. It's quite cold, but the sky is clear. I feel the chilly air on my skin, but I'm grateful for the warm sunshine.

Today, we finally removed the scaffolding, as Mr. Ito has finished applying plaster to the exterior walls. The scaffolding will be reused indoors for painting and plastering in high places.

The wainscot panels have yet to be attached, but the kominka without the scaffolding looks neat and clean.

Mr. and Mrs. Komai are pruning the grapevines in the neighboring vineyard in preparation for a rich harvest next year and to prevent branches breaking off before the snow comes.

Lumbering Precious Jindai Keyaki
December 23, 2010. Sunny

This will be a momentous day.

In late September, we bought rare jindai keyaki from Mr. Ichimura in Joetsu. Today, Mr. Masami Shiono from Shiono Lumber Co., Ltd. in Katsunuma will cut it to make two shelves on which to place items like sake cups, teacups, and a teapot in the gallery room next to the earthen floor. Mr. Shiono is the second generation to run his family's lumber mill. I have faith in him to do an excellent job.

On the way from Yokohama to Yamanashi, I stopped the car in the Hatsukari parking area and enjoyed a most beautiful scene: Mt. Fuji crowned with snow in full sunlight. It's significant that the weather should be so good on the day we cut such valuable wood.

This is my thirty-fifth visit to Yamanashi this year. Looking back, I have always been blessed with good weather. "I'm a sunny guy after all," I think to myself, "and the heavens are blessing the kominka." I am always happy when I think like this.

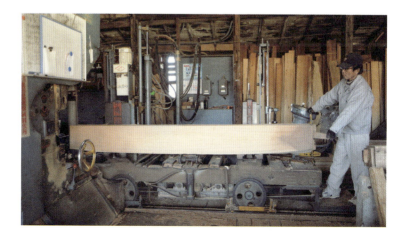

The saw blades, shaped like belts about eight to nine yards long, are set in the machine when I arrive. The first lumbering to be done is for the hidana grate that will hang above the earthen floor. Careful discussions are held on how to chamfer the edges of the old keyaki materials that were formerly used as pillars. Then, the lumbering begins.

Next, the old keyaki materials that were once beams are cut to make the entrance sliding doors. After this, it's finally time for jindai keyaki to take the stage.

I am not surprised when the seasoned professionals working on the project say that, even with their decades of experience, they are seeing jindai keyaki for the first time. Mr. Nozawa had the same reaction when he first saw the wood!

I wonder what kind of grain will appear. Will it meet our expectations? "It's possible that the cut wood will be weathered

Clockwise from top left: Mr. Shiono and Mr. Nozawa discuss how best to chamfer the edges; the blade enters the jindai keyaki; a magnificent wood grain appears

and damaged," Mr. Nozawa says, trying to prepare us for disappointment.

Tension fills the workshop as the blade enters the jindai keyaki, which has been buried in the ground for thousands, maybe tens of thousands of years. We all hold our breath before releasing a sigh of relief.

A magnificent wood surface resembling tarnished silver appears. The deep, subdued color is awesome. The professionals gaze at the wood grain and murmur, "Mmm." They are speechless.

Then, Mr. Shiono said quietly, "It's amazing! There won't be another chance to lumber this kind of keyaki again!" But then he added, "It's too precious for a kominka. It should be used for a tea room or high-end furniture." I thought to myself, "No, it's perfect for a kominka!" But I didn't say it out loud. In any case, I was truly impressed by the excellent work I witnessed. It was my first time seeing lumbering up close, so it had an even bigger impact on me.

After finishing the work, we took a commemorative photo with jindai keyaki in the middle. Everyone wore a big, wonderful smile.

Closing Out Work in 2010

December 28, 2010. Sunny

This year, which has been focused on the restoration of the kominka, is coming to an end. Today is the last day of work in 2010. It's a clear winter day. Despite the coldness, which makes you almost want to ask for a little bit of the scorching heat of summer to return, the weather is refreshing and invigorating.

In the initial plan, the restoration was scheduled to be completed by the end of October. However, due to our decision to take our time and not rush the project, construction has been delayed. At this pace, it looks like we won't be able to move in until next spring. But that's all right. Our aim is to create a house that can be lived in for at least a hundred, maybe 200 years. So, rather than hurry, we will continue to enjoy the process.

Over the past year, everyone on the site, including Mr. Nozawa, has done an excellent job. Thank you! Thank you! Thank you!

Although there have been some minor problems, it is a blessing that we are able to close out work for the year without any accidents. Despite today being the last day of work, everyone is working steadily, as always.

2011—FINISHING THE JOB
Back to Work
January 6, 2011. Clear skies

Today is the first day back to work after the New Year. The weather is beautiful, and Mt. Fuji looks incredible. We have put up New Year's decorations at the entrance and pray for the safe completion of the project. We took a commemorative photo.

In normal companies and government offices, the first day back to work in January usually ends in the morning, after everyone has greeted and wished each other well. But we are in full swing on the site. The main task for today is painting the upper beams and columns inside the house, using the repurposed scaffolding.

New Year's decorations

After lunch, I noticed that the painters were sound asleep in their cars, probably recovering from fatigue caused by the job or maybe from drinking too much sake during the New Year's celebrations.

In any case, let's hope construction proceeds smoothly and safely this year, and we can complete it without any accidents.

Clockwise from top: Ringing in the New Year with a photo; the painters may have drunk too much sake over the holiday; scaffolding inside the house

Reimagining the Earthen Floor
January 9, 2011

Flexibility and a willingness to incorporate new ideas and elements are essential when renovating a kominka. For example, the earthen floor usually serves as the house's entranceway, but we want to use ours as a gallery or event space in the future. With this in mind, we have put extra effort into designing the space, choosing the right materials, and selecting lighting to make the space versatile.

We thought of using stone for the earthen floor. However, it was difficult to find a type of stone that matched the image we had in mind, and we had to visit many suppliers before finally settling on a stone from South America called Quartz Black. At first glance, it looks like a kind of slate, but it is much darker and has a rougher texture.

Mr. Mitsuru Watanabe, the president of Watanabe Tile Industry, tiled the stone. Although handling the stone was a little tricky, he did an amazing job with the installation.

Above, Quartz Black; *right*, an irori hearth has been installed in the earthen floor space

What Is Black Plaster?

January 17, 2011. Sunny

With the painting of the woodwork inside the building complete, the plastering of the interior walls can begin. The sakan (plasterer) is the same Mr. Shinobu Ito who plastered the exterior walls. He works carefully and steadily. As there is quite a lot of wall space, it will take him about two weeks to plaster everything.

While most walls will be covered with white plaster, the tokonoma alcove on the first floor and some other surfaces will be covered with black plaster. Black plaster is usually made by mixing pine smoke or ink with the plaster, but a special technique—devised by Mr. Nozawa, the master builder—will be used in this kominka. Iron sand is to be mixed with the plaster. I am told that this innovative black plaster will increase in appeal over time. I look forward to experiencing that.

After the undercoat dries, a final coat of black plaster is applied

Fine-tuning the Exterior

January 19–21, 2011. Sunny

The stones that will surround the exterior walls have been delivered. We will supplement these with stones excavated from the site. Simultaneously, the wainscot panels are being installed and the exterior walls are being painted. A lot going on!

Top, delivering the large and heavy boulders that will surround the house. *Above from left,* painting an exterior wall; installing wooden paneling; positioning the boulders

The Tokonoma Alcove
January 27, 2011

From the outset, it has been our intention to incorporate my son's artworks into various parts of the house and harmonize them with the traditional atmosphere.

His first challenge was to create a unique piece for the tokonoma alcove in the keyaki room. The design—an iron pillar with a special dark brown rust color and an embedded light—boldly cuts out the space behind the staircase with a golden glow. It is a fascinating artwork.

Due to tight schedules, the piece could only be installed at night. Once it was in place, the plasterer Ito, who had been waiting patiently, began to apply black plaster mixed with iron sand. The collaboration between carpenter, plasterer, and metal artist is nearly complete.

Clockwise from top left: Hajime installing an iron pillar; Mr. Ito applying black plaster; the completed alcove

In Praise of Shadows

January 27, 2011. Sunny

To emphasize the Japanese ambience of the kominka, we decided to install shoji screens on all windows. In this, I totally identify with Junichiro Tanizaki and his masterpiece, *Inei Raisan* (In Praise of Shadows). The shadows and softness created by the diffusion of light through Japanese paper bring a feeling of serenity and comfort. It is gentle on the eyes and soothes the soul. And this uniquely Japanese "beauty" is also practical. Shoji screens made

from washi paper, when combined with double-glazed windows, provide excellent insulation.

Four six-foot-wide sliding glass doors have been installed in the south-facing living room to maximize the view. To match the size of these large glass doors, I designed snow- and moon-viewing shoji screens to be placed inside of them. The typical width of traditional shoji screens is three feet, so you don't often see screens as large as these.

We asked Miyazaki Woodworking to make these screens. At our initial meeting at the end of last year, Mr. Miyazaki, the owner of the shop, tilted his head and said, "I've never made such a large

Making shoji screens at Miyazaki Woodworking

shoji screen before, especially for snow viewing. It will inevitably lose its shape when it gets wet. It's better not to make a screen this size."

However, this shoji screen design is an important element in the restoration. We cannot compromise, and so I pushed back, saying, "Please challenge yourself, even if it's difficult."

Soon after the New Year, Mr. Miyazaki called me and said, "I still can't make that large screen. I want to withdraw from the project."

Slightly angry and disappointed, I asked a carpenter friend of mine to take on the job, and I called Mr. Nozawa to inform him of the change. But a few days later, Mr. Nozawa contacted me and said, "Could you give Miyazaki Woodworking another chance? He's definitely skilled, but he's a cautious type. I immediately contacted him after your call and reprimanded him. How could he refuse when the client had given him the opportunity to try something new?! Is he a craftsman?!" Apparently, Mr. Miyazaki was quite upset.

I think he probably declined the job because his conscientious work ethic won't allow him to take on a commission he's not confident he can do well.

But in the end, after all that fuss, Mr. Miyazaki accepted the challenge and made the large shoji screens—after I tinkered with the design to minimize warping and made some adjustments to the way the washi paper would be attached. The screens turned out to be a huge success.

Meticulously Designed Bathroom Facilities
February 8, 2011

I have given a lot of thought to the design of the bath. To put it somewhat dramatically, I want this bath to be the culmination of all the memorable baths that I have experienced and enjoyed in overseas hotels and Japanese hot springs and ryokans. To that end, I have placed it in the best spot in the house, with a view of Mt. Fuji and the cityscape through a large picture window. I know it won't be as luxurious or as large as what I imagine a king's bath to be, but I am determined that it will be comfortable and big enough to stretch out in and relax—no matter how much hot water it takes to fill it.

I personally drew up the specific requirements for the tub—its height and depth, as well as the thickness and size of its rim—and handed them over to the master carpenter who crafted it from the magnificent Izu stone that I brought from the Izu area.

The materials for the bathroom itself are solid Japanese cypress and Quartz Black (the same as we are using for the earthen floor). Thick cypress boards have been placed around the edge of the bathtub like a bench; I imagine myself taking a sip (or two) of

sake from the flask and cup that I will place on this surface. The fragrance of cypress permeates the air.

Thanks to everyone's efforts, the bath has been completed as envisioned.

Immediately afterward, work on the washroom and toilet began. We had in mind a design that was simple and modern, yet timeless. To that end, we opted for a toilet with Japan's renowned washlet function. But selecting the rest—washbasins, faucets, mirrors, and other fixtures—which I thought would be easy, turned out to be quite challenging, no matter how many manufacturers' showrooms we visited. We reluctantly explored options from overseas as well, eventually choosing a washbasin and faucet from Duravit in Germany, and a urinal from Allia in France.

For the first-floor toilet, Mr. Watanabe made a custom washbasin using the remaining Izu stone from the bath. It has a charm that you almost never find in ready-made products, or so I believe. Also, we used what was left of the jindai keyaki for a one-of-a-kind washstand. What a luxurious choice!

For the sink in the second-floor toilet, we found a large ceramic basin during a trip to Gifu, drilled a hole in it, and placed it in a washstand made with leftover keyaki wood.

For the washroom mirror, we took parts from IKEA and covered them with solid cedar boards, giving a calm and refined finish. We also incorporated antique fittings for the doors of the washroom and toilet, as well as for the cabinet doors in the toilet.

Opposite page: The one-of-a-kind bathtub boasts an equally one-of-a-kind view.
This page, clockwise from top left: The completed washroom; special hardware designed and made by Hajime; the washstand's custom Izu stone basin and jindai keyaki surface; antique fittings lend further distinction to the washstand; the first-floor toilet; the ceramic sink in the second-floor toilet

The Loft

February 22, 2011

Master carpenter Kusunoki works without referring to the blueprints

One of the highlights of this project has been the addition of the loft space. The original house was a single-story structure, but we raised the roof to create a large loft and an open space with a high ceiling. This is one of the boldest adjustments that we have made, and it was for me the most exciting and enjoyable part of

Top, left and right, the loft handrails before being painted. *Above,* the finished loft

renovating the kominka. The idea for the loft came from Karl, who worked with me on the design. Skilled carpenter Homare Kusunoki is crafting the loft's handrails. With years of experience, he works quickly and efficiently without even needing to refer to the blueprints.

Another Meticulously Designed Space—the Kitchen
February 26, 2011

In traditional Japanese houses, kitchens usually face north, the reason being that it is a cold, sunless exposure and food would therefore not spoil. If built facing south, the kitchen would be hot and uncomfortable in the summer and food would spoil. That is the conventional wisdom. But I decided to challenge the taboo. If the kitchen is in a bright and sunny place with a good view, I reasoned, wouldn't cooking be even more enjoyable? And I like to cook. So, our kominka's kitchen faces south and Mt. Fuji, just like the bath. The kitchen is where the entrance used to be in the original house.

I started out by visiting showrooms, where models of kitchens were on display. But when I heard the prices, I was shocked at how expensive they were. Not at all within my budget. And the quality didn't match the price. I soon realized that we would have to make our own kitchen. But I am completely clumsy. On the other hand, my son, an artist, specializes in making things. He expressed an interest in constructing a rational, practical, and easy-to-use kitchen

Mt. Fuji, the Kofu Basin, and Enzan, as seen from the kitchen windows

based, in part, on his overseas travels and experience as a visiting artist at the Glasgow School of Art in Scotland.

With my rough sketch of a floor plan as his guide, Hajime created precise digital blueprints on his computer, showing the size of the countertop and its height, and the placement of the sink and IH appliances. We also allocated ample space for storing cooking utensils and dishes, as well as a large trash can and recycling bins.

The standard height for kitchen countertops in Japan is typically thirty-three inches, but my son suggested making it thirty-five inches. Young people in Japan are apparently growing taller! We also designed the kitchen to be a bit wider, integrated the washing machine into the kitchen unit, and incorporated a slightly larger sink. We wanted to build in a refrigerator, but we couldn't find a suitable one and had to abandon that idea. We decided to use Corian, a surfacing material developed by DuPont, for the countertop, which my son installed.

Some of the components, such as drawers for storing cooking utensils and dishes, were sourced from IKEA. But my son couldn't find any drawer handles he liked from IKEA, so he custom-made his own, engraving favorite sayings, mottos, or quotes on the hardware. Phrases like:

> "Without tasting the finest wines of life, what's the point of living?"
> "Let it be! So be it!"
> "There's no such thing as being too late to do something."
> "Don't think of the time spent drinking wine as wasted. Your mind is resting!"
> "Alcohol is life's biggest enemy. However, it is written in the Bible, 'Love your enemy.'"
> "No amount of gold can buy freedom."

AUTHOR'S NOTE: At this writing, my son has been so busy that he has not been able to engrave all the handles. Someday.

In addition to the wall-mounted counter, I had initially envisioned an additional L-shaped counter along the window side of the spacious kitchen area. But since there is a pillar in the middle of the room, I changed my mind and decided to create an island surrounding the pillar that not only serves as a workspace but also functions as a dining table.

For the island tabletop, I repurposed the thick keyaki wood that was originally used in the kominka's tokonoma (elevated alcove). This beautiful keyaki wood is easily between 300 and 400 years old and has been in use for over a century. When planing the wood, beautiful grain patterns emerge, accompanied by a pleasant

Top, left and right, Hajime working on the kitchen; *above left,* the kitchen when still a work in progress; *above right,* beautiful grain patterns emerge when keyaki wood is planed by hand

The completed kitchen

fragrance. It's fascinating how wood can remain alive even after hundreds of years. The island was completed in about ten days.

I have to praise my son. He worked around the clock (or so it seemed), bringing a sleeping bag to the construction site to save travel time and transportation costs from Yokohama. When I saw the finished room, I was honestly surprised by the professional-level quality. Plus, by doing the work himself, he crafted it for less than a quarter of the cost of a prefab kitchen from a major manufacturer! I am truly satisfied.

Paving the Entrance

March 1, 2011. Light rain

Today was cold and rainy. But that didn't prevent a major task from being completed.

Initially, there was no plan for stone paving at the entrance to the house. However, the master carpenter, Mr. Nozawa, suggested that such paving would be appropriate for a traditional kominka. Conveniently, he had stones at his construction yard that we could use. As we found out, some weighed several tons! But a large crane and truck handled the load.

Once the largest stone was carefully positioned to ensure it was level and in the right spot, we moved on to medium-sized stones. We also selected flat stones from those that had been excavated when the site was leveled. The stones fit perfectly.

Before I knew it, the job was done, and it was only midmorning. I thought it would take all day, but that's what happens when you work with professionals.

A Winter Wonderland

March 7, 2011. Snow

It was snowing when I arrived at the site this morning. For those like me who live in a city, a snowy landscape is a delight. But this was even more special. As I drove through the falling snow, the sight of my kominka in the distance was truly beautiful. By evening, the snow had stopped; and as the sun set, it shone on the lightly covered landscape.

Great East Japan Earthquake
March 11, 2011

A magnitude-9.0 earthquake struck the Japanese archipelago today at 2:46 p.m.

The epicenter stretched across a vast area of approximately 300 miles north to south, from off the coast of Iwate Prefecture to off the coast of Ibaraki Prefecture, and over 100 miles east to west, making it the strongest earthquake in Japan's recorded history.

I was working at my desk in my apartment in Yokohama. The tremors were incredibly intense, unlike anything I had ever experienced before. I couldn't move. For a moment, I thought, "Is this finally the successor to the Great Kanto Earthquake of 1923?" I held on to my desk.

The shaking continued without any signs of subsiding, although it was probably just tens of seconds. I realized that it might be dangerous to stay indoors. Luckily, my apartment is on the first

My apartment in Yokohama during the earthquake

floor. So, I opened the sliding glass door and rushed out into the garden. The tremors persisted, and both the building and the ground shook and swayed.

Although my Yokohama apartment is said to have a bearing wall structure and was designed to withstand earthquakes, I still couldn't help but think, "The building might collapse, and I might die." I genuinely feared for my life.

I later heard from the master carpenter, Mr. Kusunoki, that the seismic activity was also incredibly intense at the restoration site in Yamanashi.

Mr. Kusunoki told me that he was finishing the ceiling in the loft area on the third floor when a strong tremor hit. He managed to steady himself by gripping one hand on the beam and the other on the handle of one of the glass windows. The shaking felt like it lasted for a long time, he said, around five to ten minutes. During that time, the wooden structures within the building were creaking and making a tremendous noise as they interacted with each other. Outside, wave-like ripples formed in the puddles, splashing water up to three feet high. This was something he would never forget.

Then, after the first wave of shaking subsided, he cautiously made his way outside with unsteady steps, only to experience another round of tremors. He was dazed. When the situation calmed down a bit, he surveyed both the inside and outside of the building. Apart from some minor cracks in the areas where the undercoat of plaster had been completed and the topcoat had only just begun to be applied, there was hardly any damage to the kominka.

Mr. Kusunoki, who is also a qualified architect of the first order, put a positive spin on the event. "It was like conducting a seismic test for the renovated kominka before its completion," he said. "The flexible structure—achieved by the traditional wooden frame construction method, combined with the use of ishibadate foundations (pillars resting on stones without being fixed)—was able to absorb and dissipate the energy of the earthquake, demonstrating its resilience."

A Promise Kept: My Very Own Moon-Viewing Deck
March 17, 2011. Sunny

I had made a solemn promise to myself that I would add a tsukimidai—outdoor moon-viewing deck—to the kominka, no matter how many people objected to the idea (and several did). For me, it was an absolute necessity. Moreover, it would have to be a decent-sized deck that wouldn't be overshadowed by the house!

Where did this obsession originate? I remember a visit to Katsura Rikyu, a Kyoto imperial villa, during my junior high school days. The moon-viewing deck there captured my imagination and stuck in my mind. How enjoyable it would be to have such a platform in my own home, I thought then. And now, many years later, I have one! While the moon-viewing deck at Katsura Rikyu faces a pond and is constructed with bamboo, exuding a refined ambience, I envisioned ours to be a more modest and rustic structure, fitting for a kominka that overlooks mountains and a town.

For the deck's flooring, we considered using imported wooden boards that can withstand exposure to water, but ultimately we went with domestically sourced Japanese cypress. According to Mr. Nozawa, cypress is water-resistant and doesn't split easily.

With the size and location of the deck determined, ishibadate stones are laid out for the foundation

Furthermore, materials are easily at hand here in Japan should repairs be necessary.

Carpenters Kusunoki and Hayakawa assembled the deck quickly.

The major carpentry work inside the house is just about done, so we can begin to sweep up wood chips and dust in preparation for painting the floors. We hope to start this afternoon.

Having Fun With Decor
March 2011

Kofukuan

I have always been attracted to antiques and vintage items, gradually collecting them over the years. But from the outset of the restoration project, I knew that I would have to step up my collecting if I were to have enough suitable furniture to complement the traditional atmosphere that we were creating. Fortunately, I stumbled upon excellent antiques shops in Machida and Hachioji in Tokyo. One such store, Kofukuan, offers a wide selection of quality antique furniture at reasonable prices, and I was fortunate enough to acquire a few of its well-preserved pieces from the Meiji period for the house.

    Things don't always go according to plan when renovating and decorating a kominka. One has to be flexible and open to new elements being added and modifications being made during the construction process. And that's where asobi kokoro—"playfulness"—comes in, allowing us to incorporate spontaneous, on-the-spot bits of creativity that are clever, often practical, sometimes whimsical, and always pleasing to the eye.

For example, we turned a small space behind the stairs, which in a typical new house would be closed off by a wall, into an open shelf. In another small space, this time in the attic and under the roofline, we inserted a bookshelf that can also be used as a bedside table. We also had fun when we repurposed an old ranma (a carved

Top, a small space behind the stairs was turned into an open shelf; *middle and above*, a bookshelf was inserted under the roofline

Going against tradition: An old ranma (carved wooden transom screen) is installed near the floor, not the ceiling

wooden transom screen) by placing it not above a door and beneath the ceiling, as is usual, but lower down the wall and near the floor where it is both decorative and a source of light.

Many mortise and tenon joints remain in our old timber pillars and beams, and while some people might choose to fill them in or eliminate them altogether, we have purposely left them as they are. They are witnesses to the craftsmanship of the original carpenters and add an invaluable historic touch to the renovated kominka. Within these joints, we have discreetly hidden small ceramic daruma dolls, wooden carvings of Jizo statues, profiles carved into small pieces of wood that we purchased during our travels abroad, iron mice, wooden cats obtained from the morning market in Katsunuma, two pigs made from small branches (charms believed to bring happiness), and more. "Playfulness" is one of the great joys of renovating a kominka.

My Kominka Odyssey and Diary 327

Playful surprises are tucked within the wooden joints

Antique Doors That Say "Welcome"

March 2011

The entrance door and the partition door, which leads from the earthen floor to the living space, are the most prominent fixtures in this building. They are, you could say, the face of the house.

As a tribute to the original kominka, I decided to use one of its two keyaki doors that were formerly used as nakado (the door just beyond the main entrance) for the entrance. Another door was redesigned and newly crafted. Even though it was new, I still wanted it to exude a certain elegance, so I chose pieces of

The entrance door

high-quality antique keyaki wood from Mr. Ichimura. Since I also wanted to incorporate bamboo into the door, I asked Mr. Tokumitsu Tsuchiya from Tsuchiya Joinery Shop in Yokohama to make it. Miyazaki Woodworking made the lattice doors that separate the earthen floor from the living space, also using my design and antique keyaki wood.

Working with old materials can be more challenging than working with new materials, but both sets of doors turned out beautifully. To achieve overall color harmony, the lattice doors were carefully painted with a traditional Kumezo coloring widely used in the Edo period (1603–1867) and then fitted into place. The results are splendid.

The partition (lattice) door

Storage, Bookshelves, Lighting

March 22, 2011

It would be disappointing to have a wonderful home but have things scattered all over the place. Because a typical Japanese house has limited space, it tends to become cluttered. To address this issue, traditional countryside houses in Japan have a main house and a separate storage building (kura). However, it was financially impractical to relocate and restore a kura on our property in Yamanashi. So, when it comes to storage, I have to be creative.

Initially, we considered using the room adjacent to the keyaki room on the first floor as a living space, but due to its northwestern location, it is more suitable for storage. At its entrance, we installed a magnificent kura door made from a single slab of keyaki wood, generously given by a friend who is a fellow kominka enthusiast. We named this storage area "Kura no Ma" ("Kura Room"). There aren't

The magnificent kura door at the entrance to the storage area named "Kura no Ma"

many things of great worth stored inside. The door itself is the most valuable treasure!

Additionally, because we raised the roof, we were able to secure a large space on the second floor. Although the ceiling height is less than five feet, it works well for storage. It can also be used as a secret room.

As someone who enjoys reading, I have a considerable collection of books. But storing them in my small apartment in Yokohama was a problem until, after much trial and error, I created what I call the "Hasegawa Modular Bookcase." The square frame measures thirty-five x thirty-five inches, has a depth of twelve inches, and no back panel. The shelves are adjustable, and all parts are made of one-inch-thick wood. I intend to replicate this unit in a long and narrow space on the north wall of the keyaki room.

Clockwise from top right: The "Hasegawa Modular Bookcase;" installing the bookcase; an antique low chest serves as a TV stand; shoji screens hide the TV when it is not in use

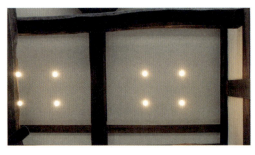

Karl insisted on installing four incandescent downlights for each one-tatami space

The challenge, however, is finding high-quality one-inch-thick lumber. On the advice of Mr. Toyoki Takeda of Takeda Construction in Hokkaido, who is also a member of the Japan Minka Revival Association, I sourced tamo (Japanese ash) lumber, which is ideal for making furniture. Mr. Kusunoki, the master carpenter, excels in woodworking, and he has just finished assembling the bookcase.

I also plan to install a television in the keyaki room, but I want to hide it when it's not in use, so I will incorporate a shoji screen on the front. When the interior light of the book unit is turned on, I can enjoy the world of *In Praise of Shadows* through the screen.

Lighting is a crucial and important element, even for a kominka. In fact, precisely because it is a kominka, I believe it requires appropriate, atmospheric, and functional lighting. Definitely not fluorescent lamps, which emit artificial and impersonal light. While it may increase the electricity bill slightly, I primarily use incandescent bulbs for all the lighting fixtures, occasionally incorporating LED bulbs that radiate soft, warm light. Additionally, dimmers have been installed throughout the house.

When it came to lighting the first-floor living area, Karl Bengs, who is a perfectionist, would not budge. He insisted on installing four incandescent downlights for each one-tatami space (the size of a tatami mat is a set standard and is approximately eighteen square feet). Both the head carpenter and I suggested that one or at most two lights per tatami would be sufficient, but Karl, based on his experience, held his ground: "No! You absolutely need four!" Because we respected Karl's opinion, we relented. And the "Beng's magic" worked once again. The space does indeed have the necessary brightness for its size.

Clockwise from top left: A lighting fixture, made from an old saw and activated by motion sensors, hangs in the earthen floor; a contemporary table lamp is whimsically set in an antique birdcage; spotlights focus attention on calligraphy and other artworks; Hajime's iron floor pillar illuminates a room with artistic flair

Painting the Floors

April 7, 2011. Sunny

The choice of paint was one of the most important aspects of this renovation. It was a matter of not only color but also health.

In the past, when a major construction company built a house for my family or when we moved into a newly constructed condominium, the children suffered from Sick Building Syndrome. At that time, Sick Building Syndrome was not yet a widely recognized issue, and its cause was unknown. We assumed Hajime and his sister Rei were suffering from allergies and had no choice but to endure them. When it was later revealed that SBS was due to the formaldehyde contained in the paint and wallpaper adhesives, it quickly became a social problem in Japan and regulations were put in place. Europe, however, had acted

From top: A pristine, solid wood floor before being painted; applying the base coat; the base coat dries before the second coat is applied

sooner. In Germany, natural and harmless materials in paints had become the norm.

When I asked Karl Bengs to work on the project with me, one of the conditions he laid down was that we only use paint that he recommended. I agreed. And so, Karl prepared a mixture of natural water-based materials sourced from Germany, and after confirming the color, we proceeded with the painting work.

At first, I regretted applying paint to the pristine, solid wood floors, but I quickly got over that. This German-made paint requires a two-step process: first, a base coat is applied and allowed to dry, followed by a second coat. Since the paint is water-based, it tends to peel off when it comes into contact with water. To prevent this, an acrylic-based topcoat is laid on. This adds a moderate sheen, giving a sophisticated and serene appearance.

It took three weeks to paint the floors, from March 17 to today.

An acrylic-based topcoat seals two undercoats of water-based paint

Cherry Blossoms at Erinji Temple

April 8, 2011. Overcast

Spring is finally here.

Erinji temple, the final resting place of Takeda Shingen, one of the most famous feudal lords during the Sengoku period in the 16th century, is just a ten-minute drive from the renovation site. When I went into town for some shopping, I passed by the temple, and the cherry blossoms were in full bloom. The sky was slightly overcast, but it actually enhanced the colors of the flowers. I stopped my car and gazed in awe. This is paradise, I thought.

Papering the Shoji Screens

April 8, 2011. Overcast

Today, Mr. Hiroshi Ota from Ota Company, specialist in interior design in Fuefuki, Yamanashi, and his wife are applying washi paper to the shoji screens. They work efficiently, and their movements are precise. I am completely mesmerized as they skillfully cover one screen after another, both large and small. Despite the considerable number of screens, they complete the task in no time.

Shoji screens offer a highly cost-effective and efficient solution to energy conservation. In combination with wooden window frames with double-glazed glass panels, they provide excellent insulation—and are aesthetically pleasing.

The Final Steps

April 15, 2011. Sunny

Today's project: installing the exterior staircase leading up to the moon-viewing deck. Originally, we had planned to use wood for the stairs, but when we were excavating for the foundation last year, we came across some sizable stones that my son suggested would make a perfect staircase. I enthusiastically jumped on board with the suggestion. But clumsy as I am, I could only watch the work unfold as my son took charge, and with Mr. Nozawa and Mr. Kusunoki used a crane to carefully lift and install the stones in their designated positions. The end result is a beautifully crafted stone staircase.

The completion ceremony is just two days away!

The Cost of Renovating the Kominka
April 2011

With the renovation of our old Japanese house nearing completion, the whole picture is becoming clearer. I'd now like to touch on the topic of renovation costs.

First, let's look at some specific numbers. While it's difficult to give an exact figure—construction costs vary depending on the size, specifications, and grade of the house, as well as regional differences—let's assume we're talking about an average wooden house with a floor area of about fifty tsubo (1,780 square feet). As of 2010, the cost of building a new house like this using typical Japanese construction methods would have been around 700,000–800,000 yen per tsubo ($140–$160 per square foot)* for a total cost of between 35 and 40 million yen.

So, how much did it cost to renovate our old Japanese house? The bottom line is that we were able to complete the renovation within the same budget as a new wooden house built using traditional construction methods and at a cost of around 700,000 yen per tsubo. This includes not only the cost of dismantling and transporting the old house, but also design fees, German-made wooden windows, screens, digging a well, and other expenses.

Our house was on the large size, so the total cost was quite high. We also added some custom features that were not part of the original plan, which extended the construction period from the proposed ten months to fourteen months and resulted in additional costs. However, considering the quality of the finished product and the fact that we were able to use rare and valuable old materials that are difficult to obtain today, I believe that the final cost was quite reasonable and satisfactory. In fact, I'm very pleased with the result and believe that this renovated kominka will continue to be used and appreciated for another century or more.

Of course, we made efforts to keep the cost down. As I have already mentioned, we challenged ourselves to undertake tasks

* US $1 = 140 yen (2023)

that we believed we could handle and endeavored to accomplish them. For example, my son took on the job of building the kitchen, which he was able to complete at approximately one-fourth of the cost of a commercially available system kitchen. I personally sourced antique fittings, old materials, and the Quartz Black stone used in the earthen floor from various places. We also searched for lighting fixtures, washlet toilets, and washbasin units that suited our taste, negotiating directly with manufacturers and using the internet to purchase them.

These actions were carried out with the understanding and support of Mr. Nozawa and the staff, which allowed us to be somewhat demanding while at the same time significantly contributing to reducing costs.

Additionally, being able to participate in the process of building a home, no matter how small the participation, not only helped reduce costs it also let me share the enjoyable experience of creating a home with the skilled craftsmen.

It is essential to mention the other important factor that contributed to the reasonable cost: the construction contract system of Nozawa Jyuken Co., Ltd., led by Mr. Nozawa, whom we entrusted with the project. According to Mr. Nozawa's calculation, the basic cost of a typical traditional house renovation project can range from around 600,000 to 650,000 yen per tsubo ($120–$130 per square foot).

It is important to note that our project involved the complete dismantling and relocation of an entire house, which resulted in comprehensive reconstruction. Had it been a case of on-site

renovation or refurbishment, the construction costs would certainly have been lower.

There are various ways to approach the renovation of old houses. For example, I have had the experience of renovating a machiya townhouse, transforming it into a charming and comfortable home without incurring significant expenses. I have even attempted to remodel an apartment interior in the style of a traditional Japanese house. My hope is that people will engage in their own way within their means.

Lastly, it's worth mentioning that the cost of construction should not be the sole determining factor. Undoubtedly, a home is one of the most significant and expensive purchases in life. Simply aiming for the cheapest option without considering quality would be unwise. On the other hand, excessively high costs that make traditional house renovation a pursuit limited to a few individuals or result in exclusive buildings would also pose significant issues. When construction costs become exorbitant, fewer people would attempt traditional house renovation, leading to the loss of these valuable cultural assets.

The reuse of traditional houses and the effective utilization of old materials were commonplace in prewar Japan. Ultimately what matters is achieving high-quality work at a reasonable cost. To accomplish this, it is crucial to collaborate with trusted designers and construction companies with rich experience and proven track records. I write this with the hope of dispelling misconceptions about kominka renovation and contributing to its broader acceptance and popularity.

Completion Day
April 17, 2011. Clear

Everyone toasts a job well done with–what else but?–Koshu wine

Finally, everyone can lay down their tools. Work is done.

I am in a reflective mood as I reminisce about my kominka journey. It has been over twenty years since I had the idea of renovating a kominka. And then there were the many years of looking for the perfect piece of land and the perfect old house to bring back to life. On July 11, 2008, I acquired half an acre in Makigaoka, Yamanashi Prefecture. A year later, I fell in love with a 100-year-old traditional Japanese house in Yasuzuka, Joetsu City, Niigata. On October 29, 2009, we started to dismantle it before transporting it here, to Yamanashi. Eighteen months have passed since then, and my idea has become a reality. The kominka, which we have named "Hideaway," is complete. Forgive me if I pat myself on the back. It is not hubris. I am truly impressed with myself—and humbled—for digging my heels in and holding on to the idea—my dream—for so long.

Yesterday, I planted a weeping cherry tree to commemorate the completion of the building. Gardening will be the next task, and hopefully the last, but today is for celebrating. We are hosting a party for all the people involved in the project.

My Kominka Odyssey and Diary 343

First, everyone gathered indoors, where I, as the client, expressed my gratitude and presented a letter of appreciation and thanks to Mr. Nozawa, the master builder, on behalf of all present. The letter was long, and I may have gone on, but everyone listened respectfully. I know they feel the same as I do about this kominka. Then, we played a DVD filmed during the construction. As I looked around the room, I wondered what master carpenter Kusunoki and Mr. Fujiwara of the Lumber Store were discussing as they watched the TV screen.

My friend Karl Bengs has come all the way from Niigata to be with us. We raised our glasses to him. With Koshu wine, of course. He reciprocated the toast by saying that although he has been on more than thirty kominka construction sites, he hasn't had many experiences as wonderful as this one.

With the formalities over, the party moves outside where the weather is nice and the barbecue has been fired up. However, before drinking too much and falling down drunk (happily), we take a photo. Everyone's expression truly captures the pleasant and harmonious atmosphere of the past year and a half.

Soon, people break off into small groups, and the air buzzes with talk. What are they saying? Does master carpenter Homare Kusunoki, who was involved in almost every aspect of the project,

Left, Mr. Nozawa and Karl Bengs flash their biggest smiles for the camera; *right*, a weeping cherry tree was planted to commemorate the end of construction

seem a little melancholic? Or am I just imagining it? Perhaps I feel a little bit lonely and sad now that everything has come to an end and all these fine craftsmen will be dispersed to other jobs and other kominka.

But I must snap out of it. This is a party! The spring sunshine is warm, and there is plenty of food, drink, and happy memories to feast on.

Former Kominka Owners' Visit

Early Summer 2011

From left, Hajime Hasegawa, Mr. and Mrs. Kazui, Mr. Nozawa

Mr. Masataka Kazui and his wife have paid a visit. Although we had exchanged letters a few times since I took over Mr. Kazui's family farmhouse in 2009, this was the first time I had the pleasure of meeting them in person.

After brief greetings, we wasted no time in touring the house, accompanied by Mr. Nozawa, the master carpenter. We began in the earthen floor gallery, where I showed them the plaque which confirmed that the original house had been built in 1911 and which Mr. Kazui had so generously given to me to keep in the revived house. We then explored the living room, hearth room, kitchen, bath, and restroom. Mr. and Mrs. Kazui could not help but express their amazement at the house's transformation, saying, "Wow, it's changed so much!"

Next, I guided them to the attic space on the second floor, which I use as my living quarters. Upon entering, both exclaimed,

Chickens were once raised in the attic room *(top)*, where I now sleep *(above)*

"Oh my!" When I asked what had surprised them, Mrs. Kazui said, "You know, back in the day, we raised chickens in this room."

I had never heard that before and wanted to know more. According to Mr. Kazui, the kominka was originally located in a heavy snowfall area, and snow would pile up as high as ten feet around the house in winter. Because of this, chickens were raised in the attic room so that they could easily come and go through its windows.

The space, when I first saw it, was a dim, dirty, and dusty attic room located above the entrance. No human had occupied it in over a decade; its only residents were bats, who left behind a considerable amount of droppings. Needless to say, my initial impression was not good.

However, as the restoration work progressed, I began to notice something interesting about the wooden framework of the room. While many traditional kominka typically used pine for the roof's framework, this particular kominka had employed massive zelkova beams, and they were assembled in a remarkably bold manner.

For me, these zelkova beams symbolized the kominka restoration project, and I decided to make this corner of the house

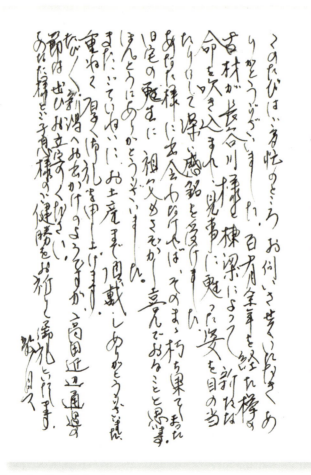

The postcard from Mr. Kazui

Mt. Fuji reflects the supermoon, as photographed from the kominka

my living space. So, now, I reside in what used to be the chicken coop! I must say, though, it is incredibly comfortable, and I am thoroughly content.

Delighted with the revitalization, Mr. and Mrs. Kazui left with satisfied smiles. Their visit was also a source of great joy for Mr. Nozawa and me.

A few days later, I received a postcard from Mr. Kazui, who wrote:

"After witnessing the magnificent revival of our old home, thanks to the efforts of Mr. Hasegawa and the master builder who used zelkova timber that had endured for over a century, I was deeply moved. If it weren't for you, this old house would have surely crumbled into obscurity. I'm certain my grandfather would be overjoyed to see it come back to life. Thank you very much."

Inspired by Mr. Kazui's heartwarming message, I have renewed my commitment to take care of this kominka and pass it on to future generations, be they a hundred or 200 years down the road.

Afterword

In 1911 (Meiji 44), a traditional Japanese farmhouse was built in one of the snowiest regions of Niigata Prefecture. Fast-forward to 2009 (Heisei 21), the year I fell instantly in love with the house and bought it with the intention of dismantling it and moving its timbers to Yamanashi Prefecture. But perhaps "bought" is too crass a word to use. The house was "entrusted" to me. I became its guardian, charged with the responsibility and privilege of restoring and giving it a new lease on life.

I have now lived in my "Hideaway" for more than a dozen years. And in that time, my attachment to it has only deepened. I can imagine living nowhere else.

Many people visit my kominka. Some are interested in learning about my experience renovating a traditional Japanese house; some are curious about the allure and challenges of living in an old house; others come seeking advice because they want to undertake their own renovation projects. I have done my best to enlighten and advise them all.

Encouraged by the enthusiasm of my visitors, I felt the need to organize and summarize the entire process for a wider audience while the memories were still fresh. Based on the diary that I kept during the restoration, I created a book, *Kominka Saisei Monogatari*, which was published in Japan in 2022. My goal was for it to be a detailed and practical how-to guide and a useful reference for anyone thinking of preserving a kominka. Now there is to be an English language version of the book, spurred on by an increased interest in Japanese architecture from abroad—fostered, in part, by UNESCO adding Japan's traditional skills and techniques for wooden construction to its Representative List of the Intangible Cultural Heritage of Humanity. I want to contribute as much as I can to the broader acceptance and popularity of kominka renovation.

Lastly, I remember with fondness and affection the many people who have made "Hideaway" a home for me. I express my gratitude to Karl Bengs for his expertise and friendship. I thank master builder Masao Nozawa and his staff for their exceptional work, including Homare Kusunoki whose demonstration of kigumi woodwork I shall never forget. I bless my children, Hajime and Rei, for their support and participation in the project. And I dedicate the house to the one person who is not here to enjoy it with me: my late wife, Chie, whose wish to live in "an old-fashioned abode"—as long as I promised that it would be the last time we would ever move—set me on this remarkable journey.

Chie and I visit Karl Bengs at Sokakuan, August 1998

古民家 ♦ *Kominka*

EXTERIOR

354　古民家 ♦ *Kominka*

ENTRANCE

My Kominka Odyssey and Diary 355

古民家 ♦ *Kominka*

EARTHEN FLOOR

My Kominka Odyssey and Diary

LIVING ROOM

LIVING ROOM

My Kominka Odyssey and Diary

KEYAKI ROOM

KITCHEN

My Kominka Odyssey and Diary 365

Clockwise from top left: The completed kitchen; the electric cooktop between the windows; ample under-the-counter storage; the Corian countertop

LOFT

My Kominka Odyssey and Diary 367

368　古民家 ♦ *Kominka*

GARDEN

Clockwise from top: Rhododendron; Genpei peach; Hyacinth orchid; Japanese enkianthus

My Kominka Odyssey and Diary 369

Clockwise from top left: Jetbead; Lilac buds; Deutzia; the path from the garden to the house's entrance; a weeping cherry tree; garden stones

Clockwise from top left: Kinome leaves add a minty flavor when added to certain dishes; aromatic Japanese pepper fruits; a ripening Nanko Ume plum; a Nanko Ume plum tree

GARDEN

Top left, Four Buddhas; *top right and above,* light snow blankets the garden

SECTIONAL DETAIL

Hideaway

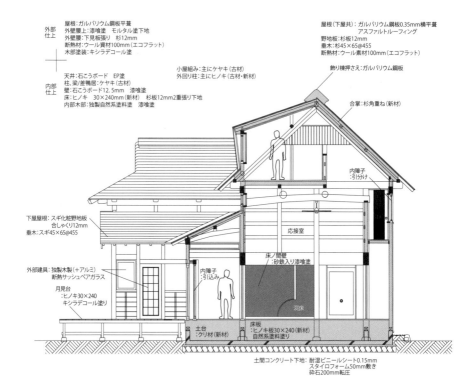

ELEVATION

FLOOR PLAN (3RD FL)

Hideaway

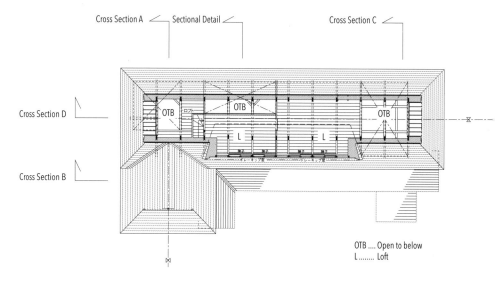

OTB .... Open to below
L .... Loft

CROSS SECTION

Cross Section A

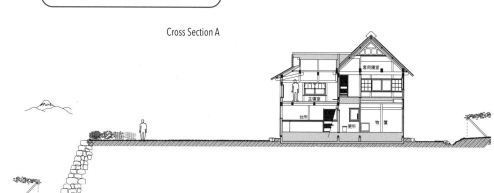

My Kominka Odyssey and Diary 377

Cross Section B

Cross Section C

Cross Section D

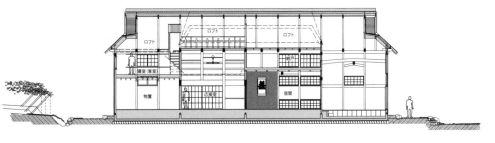

FLOOR PLANS

Kazui Family House

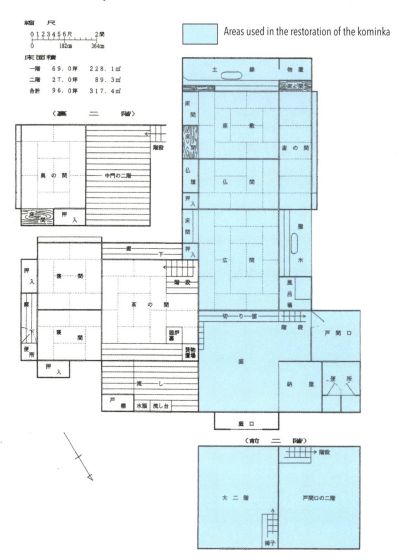

Hideaway

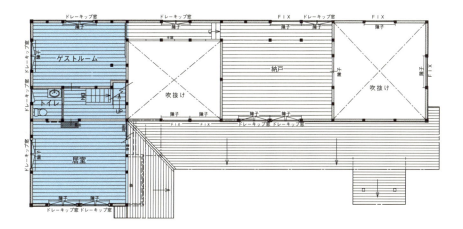

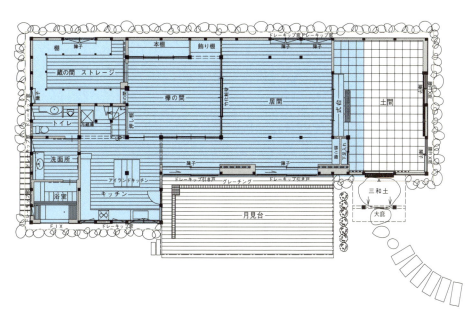

The Genius of Kigumi Carpentry

For centuries, shrines, temples, and kominka in Japan have been built using the timber frame construction method. To realize this traditional architecture, unique and advanced woodworking techniques and hand tools were developed. Still in use today, these techniques and tools are essential when restoring masterpieces like Horyuji and abodes like my "Hideaway."

The technique of kigumi woodworking—"kigumi" refers to the joining and interlocking of wood pieces—is best represented by two of the most basic types of joints: "tsugite" in which two pieces of wood are connected vertically or lengthwise and "shiguchi" in which two or more pieces of wood are joined either at an angle or in different directions. For examples of kigumi carpentry in my "Hideaway," see photographs on pp. 258, 262, 264–265, and 273–275.

Variations on kigumi carpentry are endless, but I have to wonder why some are so complicated. No doubt many were invented by carpenters to show off their skill, while others are the result of a "playful" spirit, an enduring and endearing component of Japanese architecture and design.

Shihokama-tsugi is among the most complex and beautiful kigumi joints. The name literally means "four-way gooseneck joint." On the opposite page, Mr. Homare Kusunoki, the master carpenter who worked on my "Hideaway," demonstrates how the pieces of this joint fit together without using nails, screws, or glue. Many will ask, "Isn't such a joint impossible?" As Mr. Kusunoki shows, the answer is no.

Opposite page, clockwise from top left: An architectural rendering of a shihokama-tsugi, courtesy of Hideo Satou; sliding two pieces of precisely carved wood together to form a shihokama-tsugi; when placed in front of a mirror, a shihokama-tsugi joint, with its resemblance to a goose's neck, is seen to be identical on all four sides; Homare Kusunoki assembles a tsugite joint

My Kominka Odyssey and Diary 381

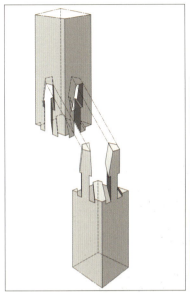

382   古民家 ◆ *Kominka*

VENUE INFORMATION

*Home pages include Japanese sites.

I

Ⓐ CHIIORI
篪庵（ちいおり）
Kominka Inn
209 Tsurui, Higashi-Iya, Miyoshi, Tokushima
https://www.chiiori-stay.jp

Ⓑ HANARE NINOUMI
離れ にのうみ
Kominka Inn
15 Nishitatsu, Kameoka, Kyoto
https://www.hanare-ninoumi.jp/home-english

Ⓒ KAWASEMI COTTAGE AND CHAYA HOTARU
カワセミ コテージ・茶屋 蛍
Kominka Inn and Cafe
1323 Kawane Sasamakami, Shimada, Shizuoka
https://www.sasuichi.org

II

❶ ESASHI TOWN
江差
Historic Town
Esashi, Hokkaido
https://en.esashi.town/

❷ KAITAKU NO MURA
開拓の村
Museum
50-1 Atsubetsu, Sapporo, Hokkaido
https://www.kaitaku.or.jp/en/

❸ KAKUNODATE
角館
Historic Castle Town
Kakunodate machi, Senboku, Akita
https://tazawako-kakunodate.com/en/area/1
https://www.city.semboku.akita.jp/en/sightseeing/spot/07.html

❹ GINZAN ONSEN
銀山温泉
Historic Hot Spring
Obanazawa, Yamagata
https://yamagatakanko.com/en/attractions/detail_2832.html

❺ OUCHIJUKU
大内宿
Historic Post Town
Shimogo-machi, Minami Aizu, Fukushima
https://ouchi-juku.com
https://www.aizu-concierge.com/feature/28005/#1

⑥ SAWARA
佐原
Historic Merchant Town
Katori, Chiba
http://www.suigo-sawara.ne.jp/abroad.html

⑦ SANKEIEN GARDEN
三溪園
Kominka Houses and Garden
58-1 Honmokusannotani,
Naka-ku, Yokohama, Kanagawa
https://www.sankeien.or.jp/en/

⑧ SADO ISLAND
佐渡島
Historic Island
Sado, Niigata
https://www.visitsado.com/en

RYOTSU OKAWA OUTDOOR WOODBLOCK PRINTS MUSEUM
大川屋外版画美術館
Outdoor Museum
Ryotsu Ogawa, Sado, Niigata
https://www.visitsado.com/en/spot/detail0012

HANANOKI INN
御宿 花の木
Kominka Inn
78-1 Shukunegi, Sado, Niigata
http://www.sado-hananoki.com

YOSABEI GUESTHOUSE
よさべい
Kominka Inn
549 Sansegawa, Sado, Niigata
https://sado-japanese-newold.jimdofree.com/

⑨ MATSUDAI BENGS HOUSE
松代ベンクスハウス
Kominka Office and Cafe
2074 Matsudai, Tokamachi, Niigata
https://www.nippon.com/en/views/b02339/
https://kb-house.com/english/

⑩ UNNOJUKU
海野宿
Historic Post Town
Tomi, Nagano
https://en.japantravel.com/nagano/history-architecture-unnojuku/43307

⑪ SANGOSO & MINAMIGAOKA ART MUSEUM
三五荘・南ヶ丘美術館
Historic Kominka and Museum
1052-7 Karuizawa, Kitasaku, Nagano
https://bunka.nii.ac.jp/heritages/detail/142008

⑫ MATSUMOTO
松本
Historic Castle Town
Matsumoto, Nagano
https://visitmatsumoto.com/en/

⑬ TSUMAGO
妻籠
Historic Post Town
Nagisomachi, Kiso, Nagano
https://tsumago.jp/en/
https://www.japan-guide.com/e/e6077.html

⑭ YAMANASHI KOMINKA CLUB
山梨古民家倶楽部
Kominka Farms, Wineries, Restaurants, and an Inn
Koshu/Yamanashi, Yamanashi
http://kominka.jpn.org/

KATSUNUMA WINERY
勝沼ワイナリー
Kominka Winery
371 Iwasaki, Katsunuma,
Koshu, Yamanashi
http://www.katsunuma-winery.com
https://www.japan-guide.com/e/e6954.html

GALLERY NASHIKIBATA
ギャラリー梨木畑
Kominka Gallery
1126 Nishihoshimo, Makioka, Yamanashi
https://wanocajitu.jp/en/shop

GALLERY WA
ギャラリー和
Kominka Gallery
484 Somaguchi, Makioka, Yamanashi
http://waso-kobo.saloon.jp

KURAMUBON WINERY
くらむぼんワイン
Kominka Winery
835 Shimoiwasaki, Katsunuma,
Koshu, Yamanashi
http://www.kurambon.com

KORYUEN ORCHARDS
興隆園
Kominka Farm
53-4 Nakamura, Yamanashi
http://www.koryuen.com

SATO BUDO
さとうぶどう
Kominka Farm
1984 Nishihoshimo, Makioka, Yamanashi
http://www.satobudo.com

SOBAMARU
そば丸
Kominka Restaurant
1756 Enzanfujiki, Koshu, Yamanashi
http://sobamaru.net

HARAMO WINERY
原茂ワイナリー
Kominka Winery
3181 Katsunuma, Koshu, Yamanashi
www.haramo.com

MARUFUJI WINERY
丸藤ワイナリー
Kominka Winery
780 Fujii, Katsunuma, Koshu, Yamanashi
http://www.rubaiyat.jp

YORO SHUZO
養老酒造
Kominka Sake Brewery
567 Kita, Yamanashi, Yamanashi
https://www.yamanashi-sake.jp/en/index-en/brewery/yoro-shuzo/

LA MAISON ANCIENNE
ラ メゾン アンシャンヌ
Kominka Restaurant
5662-5 Kurashina, Makioka, Yamanashi
http://www.ancienne-jp.com

SUZUKIEN GUESTHOUSE
ワイン民宿鈴木園
Kominka Inn
3284 Katsunuma, Koshu, Yamanashi
http://www.jalan.net/yad374324/

⓯ SHIRAKAWAGO & GOKAYAMA
白川郷・五箇山

OGIMACHI (SHIRAKAWAGO)
荻町（白川郷）
Gassho-zukuri Farmhouses
Ohno, Gifu
https://shirakawa-go.gr.jp/en/

AINOKURA, SUGANUMA (GOKAYAMA)
相倉・菅沼（五箇山）
Gassho-zukuri Farmhouses
Nanto, Toyama

https://gokayama-info.jp/en/
https://toyama-bunkaisan.jp/en/pickup/world02.php

⓰ HIDA TAKAYAMA & HIDA FURUKAWA
飛騨高山・飛騨古川
Historic Castle Town
Hida, Gifu
https://www.hida.jp/english/index.html

⓱ SEKIJUKU
関宿
Historic Post Town
Kizaki-Nakamachi-Shinjo, Sekimachi, Kameyama, Mie

https://www.kankomie.or.jp/en/report/detail_246.html

⓲ SANNEIZAKA
産寧坂
Historic Temple Town
2-221 Kiyomizu, Higashiyama, Kyoto
https://bunka.nii.ac.jp/heritages/detail/125134

Venue Information

RYOKAN UEMURA
旅館うえむら
Kominka Inn
*Gionshimokawara Ishibekoji,
Higashiyama, Kyoto*
https://ryokanuemura.jphotel.site/en/

19 MIYAMA TOWN
美山町
Kominka Farms
*Mitamacho,
Nantan, Kyoto*
https://www.japan-guide.com/e/e3985.html
http://miyamafandb.jp/

20 INE TOWN
伊根町
Historic Fishermen's Village
Yosa, Kyoto
https://www.japan-guide.com/e/e3996.html

21 TAMBA SASAYAMA
丹波篠山
Historic Castle Town
Hyogo
https://tourism.sasayama.jp/
https://matcha-jp.com/en/sasayama

HOTEL NIPPONIA
ホテル ニッポニア
Kominka Inn
25 Nishimachi, Tanbasasayama, Hyogo
https://www.sasayamastay.jp/en/

22 IMAICHO
今井町
Historic Temple Town
Kashihara, Nara
https://www.visitnara.jp/destinations/area/imaicho/

23 KURASHIKI
倉敷
Historic Port Town
Kurashiki, Okayama
https://www.japan-guide.com/e/e5750.html
https://en.japantravel.com/okayama/kurashiki-city

24 FUKIYA
吹屋
Historic Mining Town
Takahashi, Okayama
https://www.japan-guide.com/e/e5781.html

㉕ SEKITEI
石亭
Kominka Inn
3-5-27 Miyahama-Onsen,
Hatsukaichi, Hiroshima
https://www.sekitei.to/en/

㉖ HAGI
萩
Historic Castle Town
Yamaguchi
https://www.hagishi.com/en
https://www.japan-guide.com/e/e6150.html

㉗ SOTODOMARI
外泊
Historic Fishermen's Village
Minami-uwa, Ainan, Ehime
https://www.town.ainan.ehime.jp/kanko/sightseeing/zekkei/ishigakinosato.html
https://en.japantravel.com/ehime/ehime-s-sotodomari-ishigaki-no-sato/37875

㉘ UCHIKO
内子
Historic Castle Town
Kitagun, Ehime
https://uchikogenic.com/en/
https://www.japan-guide.com/e/e5550.html

㉙ KIRAGAWA
吉良川
Historic Town
Kiragawa, Muroto, Kochi
https://visitkochijapan.com/en/see-and-do/10008

KURAKUKAN KURAJUKU
蔵空間蔵宿
Kominka Inn and Cafe
2234 Ko, Kiragawa, Muroto, Kochi
http://sakan805.boy.jp/
https://higashi-kochi.jp/en/accommodation/detail.php?id=57

Venue Information 389

30 KITSUKI
杵築
Historic Castle Town
Kitsuki, Oita
https://www.kit-suki.com/eng/
https://www.japan-guide.com/e/e4725.html

31 SANSOU MURATA
山荘無量塔
Kominka Inn
1264-2 Yufuin, Kawakami, Yufu, Oita
www.sansou-murata.com/e/index.html

32 TAKETOMI ISLAND
竹富島
Historic Town
Taketomi,
Yaeyama, Okinawa
https://www.japan-guide.com/e/e7250.html

33 HAKODATE MOTOMACHI
函館元町
Historic Port Town
Hakodate, Hokkaido
https://www.hakodate.travel/en/top7/motomachi

34 OTARU CANAL
小樽運河
Historic Port Town
Otaru, Hokkaido
https://livejapan.com/en/in-hokkaido/in-pref-hokkaido/in-otaru/article-a1000081/

35 KUROYU ONSEN INN
黒湯温泉
Historic Hot Spring
2-1 Tazawakoobonai kuroyuzawa,
Senboku, Akita
http://ryokan.glocal-promotion.com/ryokan/kuroyu/

NYUTO ONSEN VILLAGE
乳頭温泉郷
Historic Hot Spring
Tazawakoobonai kuroyuzawa,
Senboku, Akita
http://ryokan.glocal-promotion.com/

36 TATEIWA VILLAGE
館岩村
Kominka Farms
Matsudohara, Minamiaizu, Fukushima
https://fukushima.travel/blogs/historic-maezawa-farmhouses-in-rural-japan/63

37 KITAKATA
喜多方
Historic Warehouses
Kitakata, Fukushima
http://www.kitakata-kanko.jp/
https://en.japantravel.com/
fukushima/kitakata

38 TOCHIGI
栃木
Historic Merchant Town
Tochigi, Tochigi
https://www.
tochigi-kankou.or.jp/
https://www.visit-tochigi.com/plan-your-trip/things-to-do/839/

39 KAWAGOE
川越
Historic Town
Kawagoe, Saitama
https://koedo.or.jp/en/

40 CHINRYUSO KYOTEI
枕流荘 京亭
Kominka Inn and Restaurant
547 Yorii, Osato, Saitama
http://chinryusou-kyoutei.jp

41 JAPAN FOLK CRAFTS MUSEUM
日本民藝館
Museum
4-3-33 Komaba, Meguro, Tokyo
https://mingeikan.or.jp/?lang=en

42 KAGURAZAKA
神楽坂
Historic Town
Shinjuku, Tokyo
https://www.
japan-guide.com/e/
e3071.html

43 TOUTOUAN
燈々庵
Kominka Restaurant
*633 Ogawa,
Akiruno, Tokyo*
https://www.tou-
touan.com/toutouan

44 HINODE SANSO / US-JAPAN SUMMIT MEMORIAL HALL
日の出山荘
Historic Kominka
5270 Oguno, Hinode-machi, Tokyo
https://medium.com/tokyo-where-history-happened/12-hinode-sanso-f507c07a224f

㊺ BUAISO

武相荘
Kominka Museum
7-3-2 Nogaya,
Machida, Tokyo
https://buaiso.com/ki/info/introduction_en

㊻ IIDA FAMILY RESIDENCE

飯田家住宅
Historic Kominka
17-5 Tsunashimadai, Kohoku,
Yokohama, Kanagawa

㊼ OGINOSHIMA VILLAGE

荻ノ島
Kominka Farms
1090-2 Oginoshima, Takayanagi,
Kashiwazaki, Niigata
https://enjoyniigata.com/en/spot/6048

OGI NO IE / SHIMA NO IE, OGINOSHIMA KAYABUKI NO YADO

荻の家・島の家
Kominka Inn
1090-2 Oginoshima, Takayanagi,
Kashiwazaki, Niigata

㊽ SANKYOSON

散居村
Historic Town
80 Taromaru, Tonami, Toyama
https://sankyoson.com/
https://zekkeijapan.com/spot/index/804/

㊾ KANAZAWA

金沢
Historic
Castle Town
Kanazawa, Ishikawa
https://visitkanazawa.jp/

㊿ KUMAGAWAJUKU

熊川宿
Historic Post Town
Wakasa, Fukui
https://www.sabakaido-traveler.com

(51) OBAMA NISHIGUMI

小浜西組
Historic Castle Town
Wakasa, Fukui
http://obama-nishigumi.sakura.ne.jp
https://www.mustlovejapan.com/subject/obama_nishigumi/

52 OSHINO VILLAGE
忍野村
Kominka Town
Shibokusa, Oshinomura, Minamitsuru, Yamanashi
https://www.japan.travel/en/spot/1327/

53 AONI
青鬼
Historic Mountain Village
Hakuba, Kitaazumi, Nagano
https://skima-shinshu.com/hakuba-aoni/
http://hakubamap.com/aoni.html

54 OBUSE
小布施
Historic Post Town
Kamitakai, Nagano
http://www.e-obuse.com/
https://www.japan-guide.com/e/e6020.html

HOKUSAI MUSEUM
北斎館
Museum
485 Obuse, Kamitakai, Nagano
https://hokusai-kan.com/en/

55 NARAIJUKU
奈良井宿
Historic Post Town
Shiojiri, Nagano
https://www.japan-experience.com/all-about-japan/nagano/attractions-excursions/narai-guide
https://www.japan-guide.com/e/e6080.htm

56 KOSHINZUKA
こうしんづか
Kominka Inn
1775 Ohtsumago, Azuma, Kiso, Nagisomachi, Nagano
https://kooshinzuka.jyunken.co.jp/english/

57 MUGEISO
無藝荘
Kominka Museum
4035 Kitayama, Tateshina, Chino, Nagano
https://www.japan-guide.com/chottozeitaku/180527.html

58 KASENAN SENI ONSEN IWANOYU
花仙庵 仙仁温泉 岩の湯
Kominka Inn
3159 Nirei, Suzaka, Nagano
https://www.suzaka-kankokyokai.jp/contents/stay/46.html
https://tei-ku.com/en/place/iwanoyu/

Venue Information 393

59 GERO ONSEN YUNOSHIMAKAN
下呂温泉 湯之島館
Kominka Inn
645 Yunoshima, Gero, Gifu
https://www.yunoshimakan.co.jp/en/

60 MINO
美濃
Historic Post Town
Mino, Gifu
https://minokanko.com/
https://en.japantravel.com/gifu/mino-city

61 NUMAZU CLUB
沼津倶楽部
Kominka Inn and Restaurant
1907-8 Senbongorin, Numazu, Shizuoka
http://numazu-club.com/index_em.html

62 IZU MATSUZAKI
伊豆 松崎
Historic Port Town
Izu, Shizuoka
https://izumatsuzakinet.com/
https://www.japan-guide.com/community/sparringenthu/report-1460

63 KAKUJORO
角上楼
Kominka Inn
38 Fukue, Tahara, Aichi
https://www.kakujoro.com/english/

64 ARIMATSU
有松
Historic Merchant Town
Midori, Nagoya, Aichi
https://www.aichi-now.jp/en/spots/detail/18/

65 ASUKE
足助
Historic Post Town
Toyota, Aichi
https://www.aichi-now.jp/en/spots/detail/118/
https://www.tourismtoyota.jp/en/spots/detail/52/

66 SHIRATAMA
志ら玉
Kominka Restaurant
2-36 Nishimachi Kamiiida, Kita,
Nagoya, Aichi
https://www.siratama.jp/en/index.html

67 SAKAMOTO
坂本
Historic Temple Town
Otsu, Shiga
https://en.biwako-visitors.jp/spot/detail/32

68 OMIHACHIMAN
近江八幡
Historic Merchant Town
Omihachiman, Shiga
https://www.city.omihachiman.lg.jp/
https://www.japan-guide.com/e/
e7075.html

69 HOTEL KOO OTSU HYAKUCHO
ホテル講 大津百町
Kominka Inn
Otsu, Shiga
https://hotel-koo.com/en/
https://otsu.or.jp/en/

70 GION SHINBASHI
祇園新橋
Historic Geisha District
Higashiyama, Kyoto
https://www.japan-guide.com/e/
e3902.html

71 SAGATORIIMOTO
嵯峨鳥居本
Historic Building District
Ukyo-ku, Kyoto
https://traditionalkyoto.com/traditional-
areas/arashiyama-district/saga-toriimoto/

72 ISHIBEKOJI
石塀小路
Kominka Inns and Restaurants
Shimokawaracho, Higashiyama, Kyoto
https://www.insidekyoto.com/
ishibei-koji-lane

Venue Information 395

73 TAWARAYA
俵屋
Kominka Inn
278 Nakahakusan, Fuya Ayanekoji-agaru, Nakagyo, Kyoto
https://icotto.jp/presses/1107

74 MO-AN
茂庵
Kominka Cafe
8 Yoshidakaguraoka, Sakyo, Kyoto
https://www.mo-an.com/
https://www.japan-experience.com/all-about-japan/kyoto/attractions-excursions/mo-an-cafe

75 KAMISHICHIKEN
上七軒
Historic Geisha District
Shinseicho, Kamigyo-ku, Kyoto
https://traditionalkyoto.com/traditional-areas/kamishichiken/

76 HIRAKATASHUKU
枚方宿
Historic Post Town
Hirakata, Osaka
https://arigatojapan.co.jp/hirakata-shuku-kagiya-museum-in-osaka-kyoto-area-unique-and-interesting-local-history-lesson-of-kurawanka-boats/

77 TAKENAKA CARPENTRY TOOLS MUSEUM
竹中大工道具館
Museum

7-5-1 Kumochi, Chuo, Kobe, Hyogo
https://www.dougukan.jp/?lang=en

78 TATSUNO
龍野
Historic Castle Town
Tatsuno, Hyogo
https://www.city.tatsuno.lg.jp/english/kankou/area.html

79 IZUSHI
出石
Historic Castle Town
Toyooka, Hyogo
https://www.japan-guide.com/community/mfedley/report-2242

🟤80 GOSE
御所
Historic Merchant/Temple Town
Gose, Nara
https://www.trip.com/travel-guide/destination/gose-57042/

🟤81 OUDA
大宇陀
Historic Post Town
Ouda, Uda, Nara
https://www.city.uda.nara.jp/shoukoukankou/kankou/kankou/jouhou/visit-to-uda-ouda.html

🟤82 RYUJIN ONSEN KAMIGOTEN
龍神温泉 上御殿
Kominka Inn
42 Ryujin, Tanabe, Wakayama
http://www.kamigoten.jp/
https://www.kumano-travel.com/en/accommodations/kamigoten-ryokan

🟤83 KURAYOSHI
倉吉

Historic Castle/Merchant Town
Kurayoshi, Tottori
https://www.japan.travel/en/spot/2296/

🟤84 MISASA ONSEN
三朝温泉
Historic Hot Spring Town
Misasa, Tohaku, Tottori
https://misasaonsen.jp/en/

KAJIKAWA'S BARBERSHOP
梶川理髪館
Kominka Barbershop
903-3 Misasa,, Tohaku, Tottori
http://barber.394u.jp/
https://en.japantravel.com/tottori/kajikawa-s-barbershop-and-museum/12891

RYOKAN OHASHI
旅館大橋
Kominka Inn
302-1 Misasa,, Tohaku, Tottori
https://www.o-hashi.net/en/

Venue Information 397

85 MATSUE
松江
Historic Castle Town
Matsue, Shimane
https://www.japan-guide.com/e/e5800.html

LAFCADIO HEARN MEMORIAL MUSEUM
小泉八雲記念館
Museum
322 Okudanicho,
Matsue, Shimane
https://www.hearn-museum-matsue.jp/english.html

86 OMORI IWAMI GINZAN
大森 石見銀山
Historic Mining Town
Omori, Ota, Shimane
https://www.kankou-shimane.com/en/destinations/9287
https://en.japantravel.com/shimane/iwami-ginzan-s-omori-cho/6818

87 TAKAHASHI
高梁
Historic Castle Town
Takahashi, Okayama
https://www.japan-experience.com/all-about-japan/okayama/attractions-excursions/takahashi

88 TOMONOURA
鞆の浦
Historic Port Town
Tomocho, Fukuyama, Hiroshima
https://www.japan-guide.com/e/e3432.html

89 ONOMICHI
尾道
Historic Port Town
Onomichi, Hiroshima
http://www.ononavi.com/
https://www.japan-guide.com/e/e3475.html

90 RYOKAN ONOMICHI NISHIYAMA
旅館 尾道西山
Kominka Inn
678-1 Sanba, Onomichi, Hiroshima
https://o-nishiyama.co.jp/?page_id=1125

🔹 WAKIMACHI MINAMIMACHI
脇町南町

Historic Merchant Town
Wakimachi, Mima, Tokushima
http://www.travel-around-japan.com/k82-06-wakimachi.html
https://en.japantravel.com/tokushima/wakimachi-minamimachi-udatsu-old-street/658

🔹 KASASHIMA TOWN
笠島

Historic Port Town
Honjima Island, Marugame, Kagawa
https://www.japan-guide.com/e/e5468.html

🔹 SHIMAYADO MARI
島宿真里

Kominka Inn
2011 Shodoshimacho-no-umakabuto, Shouzu, Kagawa
http://eng.mari.co.jp/en/
https://www.undiscovered-japan.com/?p=5203

🔹 YUSUHARA
梼原

Town That Celebrates Innovation
Yusuhara, Takaoka, Kochi
https://en.japantravel.com/kochi/yusuhara/60595

🔹 YANAGAWA
柳川

Historic Castle Town
Yanagawa, Fukuoka
https://www.yanagawa-net.com/en/

🔹 TACHIBANA-TEI OHANA
立花邸 御花

Historic Samurai Mansion
1 Shinhokamachi, Yanagawa, Fukuoka
https://en.japantravel.com/fukuoka/ohana-estate-and-villa/18694

Venue Information 399

97 TAKEGAWARA ONSEN
竹瓦温泉

Historic Public Bath
16-23 Motomachi, Beppu, Oita
https://en.japantravel.com/oita/takegawara-onsen/22298

DOGO ONSEN HONKAN (BOTCHAN'S HOT SPRING)
道後温泉本館
Historic Public Bath
5-6 Dogoyunomachi, Matsuyama, Ehime
https://www.dogo.or.jp/pc/time/
https://www.japan-guide.com/e/e5502.htm

KATAKURAKAN
片倉館
Historic Public Bath
4 -1-9 Kogandori, Suwa, Nagano
https://japantravel.navitime.com/en/area/jp/spot/02301-2000215/

98 USUKI
臼杵
Historic Castle Town
Usuki, Oita
https://www.japan-guide.com/e/e4740.html

99 GAJOEN
雅叙苑
Kominka Inn
4230 Makizono Shukukubota, Kirishima, Kagoshima
https://gajoen.jp/en/

100 IZUMIFUMOTO
出水麓
Historic Castle Town
Fumoto, Izumi, Kagoshima
https://www.japan.travel/en/spot/508/

CHIRAN
知覧

Historic Castle Town
Chiran, Minamikyushu, Kagoshima
https://chiran-bukeyashiki.com/pages/10/

CHIRAN PEACE MUSEUM
知覧特攻平和会館
Museum
17881 Kori, Chiran, Minamikyushu, Kagoshima
https://www.chiran-tokkou.jp/en/
https://www.japan.travel/en/spot/608/

III

D KAZUI FAMILY RESIDENCE
數井家住宅
Kominka
Yasuzuka, Joetsu, Niigata

E HIDEAWAY
ハイダウェイ
Kominka
Somaguchi, Makigaoka, Yamanashi

ACKNOWLEDGMENTS

Publishing a book can be compared to restoring a kominka in this respect: Both require teamwork. Fortunately, I have been able to collaborate with two dedicated teams of professionals in this, my first English-language project. They have guided me through the process with patience and care. Quite simply, this book would not have been possible without them.

First, I would like to thank my team in Japan: Mie Shimomura for collecting and organizing the names, addresses, and websites in the extensive 101 section; and architects Nobuyuki Arai and Hideo Satou for providing the book's detailed floor plans, cross sections, and elevations. I am also grateful to Alex Kerr and Shelley Clarke for agreeing to be interviewed by me and for warmly welcoming me to their kominka; I have happy memories of spending time with them, sharing our love for kominka and Old Japan.

Finally, my sincerest thanks go to Team Museyon in New York City, including Akira Chiba, my old friend, former colleague, and publisher of Museyon; Alex Child for translating my Japanese into idiomatic English; Francis Lewis for his skillful editing throughout; Mariko Garbi for her fact-checking; and Iam Imai of EPI Design Network for creating the beautiful maps and kominka illustrations.

If I think of this book as the equivalent in words and images to kigumi woodworking, in which individual pieces magically interlock, it is because of everyone's efforts on my behalf.

Photo Credits

All photographs are © Kazuo Hasegawa, except the following on p. 61: interior Aoyagi samurai family residence, courtesy of JNTO; p. 70: Misawaya restaurant, courtesy of JNTO; p. 155: Fukiya Village main street, Fukiya post office, and roofs with Sekishu clay tiles, © Okayama Prefectural Tourism Federation

INDEX

A

Agency for Cultural Affairs 12, 55
Aichi 59, 213, 214, 393, 394
Aikawa 82
Ainan 164, 165, 166, 168, 388
Ainu 53
Aizu-Wakamatsu 69
Aki 174
Akita 60, 61, 62, 193, 383, 389
Allia 310
American 20, 26, 30
Aoni 189, 205, 392
Aoyama family house 57
Arakawa River 197
Arimatsu 189
Asahi Kominka and Antique Fittings Center 282
Asuka period 15
Asuke 189, 214
Atago Shrine 218
Awa indigo dye 231
Ayabe 24

B

bamboo 322, 329
barbecue 270, 271, 343
bengara 123, 153, 154
Bengara Lantern Festival 154
Bengs, Karl 85, 87, 88, 89, 91, 248, 249, 253, 260, 264, 277, 287, 288, 313, 332, 335, 343, 351
Bengs House 50, 87, 248, 277, 384
Bering Sea 26
Berlin 88
Bikan Historical Quarter 150, 151
Bitchu Kagura 154
Bitchu-Matsuyama Castle 228
Bitchu-Takahashi 228
black plaster 74, 303, 305
Buaiso 188, 200, 391
Buddhism 144

C

Cambridge University 200
Cape Muroto 173
castle town 61, 62, 69, 93, 123, 141, 162, 163, 178, 196, 204, 215, 228, 233, 237
Castle Town 62, 100, 102, 122, 141, 142, 143, 161, 163, 176, 179, 383, 384, 386, 387, 388, 389, 391, 395, 396, 397, 398, 399, 400
cedar 18, 36, 248, 260, 266, 280, 283, 284, 311
Chiba 72, 75, 282, 384
Chiiori 7, 20, 22, 23
Chinryuso Kyotei 188
Chiran 191, 237, 400
Chuo Expressway 272
Chuo Main Line railroad 104
Chuo Mingei 103
Clarke, Shelley 7, 19, 26, 27, 30
cocoon silk 231
Commodore Matthew Perry 192
Corian 315, 365
cypress 18, 36, 112, 260, 280, 309, 310, 322

D

daimyo 114, 126
Dogo Onsen Honkan 191, 235, 399
Dogs and Demons: The Fall of Modern Japan 20
DuPont 315
Duravit 310
Düsseldorf 89

E

earthquake 320, 321
Echigo 249
Edo 13, 23, 36, 69, 71, 73, 74, 83, 85, 93, 95, 96, 100, 104, 106, 111, 114, 115, 118, 123, 124, 126, 129, 134, 141, 143, 144, 147, 148, 150, 153, 154, 166, 169, 176, 192, 195, 196, 199, 200, 204, 206,

207, 211, 214,
215, 218, 228,
231, 233, 237,
252, 285, 329
Edo period *13, 23, 36, 69,
73, 74, 83, 85, 93,
96, 100, 104, 106,
111, 114, 115,
118, 126, 134,
141, 143, 147,
148, 153, 154,
166, 169, 176,
192, 196, 199,
200, 204, 206,
207, 211, 214,
228, 231, 233,
237, 252, 285, 329*
Ehime *164, 166, 168, 171,
235, 388, 399*
Enzan *96, 265, 266, 279,
292, 314*
Erinji *114, 292, 336*
Esashi *53, 55, 383*

F

*Fifty-three Stations of the
Tokaido* (1833–34)
124
Fishermen's Village *139,
166, 387, 388*
France *310*
Fujiwara, Kazushige *281*
Fujiwara Lumber Store *280,
281*
Fukiya *51, 152, 153, 154,
155, 387*
Fukuchiyama *24*
Fukushima *68, 69, 70, 194,
195, 383, 389, 390*
funaya *137, 138*

G

Gajoen *191, 236, 399*
Gallery Nashikibata *111,
385*
Gallery Wa *111, 385*
galvanized steel *276, 277*
gassho-style *78, 118, 119*
geiko *218, 221*
geisha *131, 143, 204, 213,
218, 221*
German *85, 87, 88, 288,
335, 339*
Germany *88, 89, 287, 288,
310, 335*
Gero Onsen *189*
Gero Onsen Yunoshimakan
189, 210, 393
Gifu *78, 116, 118, 119,
120, 121, 122,
210, 211, 277,
310, 386, 393*
Ginza *245*
Ginzan Onsen *50, 64,
66, 67*
Ginzan River *67, 227*
Gion *131, 190, 217, 394*
Gion Shinbashi *190, 217,
394*
Glasgow School of Art *315*
Gokayama *50, 116, 118,
119, 386*
Gose *190, 224, 396*
Great Kanto Earthquake
320
groundbreaking ceremony
252, 259

H

Hachioji *324*

Hagi *51, 160, 161, 162,
163*
Hakodate Motomachi *188*
Hakuba *205, 392*
Hamasaki district *162*
Hanagasa Odori *67*
Hananoki Inn *85, 384*
Hanare Ninoumi *20, 25*
Haramo Winery *114, 385*
Hara Sankei *77, 78, 79*
Hasegawa, Chie *5, 242,
243, 244, 351*
Hasegawa, Hajime *5, 243,
244, 245, 259,
260, 305, 311,
315, 316, 333,
334, 346, 351*
Hasegawa, Rei *5, 334, 351*
Hasegawa Modular Book-
case *331*
Hatsukaichi *156*
Herring Palaces *55*
Hida Folk Village *123*
Hida Furukawa *50, 120,
121, 122, 123, 386*
Hida Takayama *50, 120,
121, 122, 123, 386*
Hideaway *342, 350, 351,
374, 376, 379, 400*
Hideshina Trading Com-
pany *282*
Higashiyama *128, 129,
130, 218, 386,
387, 394*
Hinode Sanso *188, 390*
hinoki *112, 260, 278*
Hinokinai River *62*
hip roof *70, 71, 266, 290*
Hirakatashuku *190*
Hirokane merchant family
153

Hiroshige *124, 127*
Hiroshima *156, 158, 228, 229, 230, 388, 397*
Hiyako district *163*
Hokkaido *21, 36, 52, 53, 55, 56, 57, 58, 59, 83, 192, 332, 383, 389*
Hokkoku Kaido *95*
Holzbau Winter GmbH *288*
Honhaga family *169, 171*
Honshu Island *124*
Horiuchi district *163*
Horyuji *15, 16, 380*
Hot Spring *65, 66, 235, 383, 389, 396*
Hotaru *30, 31*
Hotel Kagetsu *103*
Hotel Koo Otsu Hyakucho *190, 216, 394*
Hotel Nipponia *51, 140, 143, 387*
Houses and People of Japan *88*
Hyogo *140, 143, 222, 223, 387, 395*

I

Ibaraki *320*
Ichimura, Shigetaro *249, 283, 284, 290, 295, 329*
Iida Family Residence *188, 200, 391*
IKEA *311, 315*
Imaicho *51, 144, 146, 147*
Imperial College London *26*
Important Preservation District for Groups of Historic Buildings *218, 224*
Important Preservation District for Groups of Traditional Buildings *62, 71, 95, 154, 173, 178, 187, 204, 211, 231, 237*
Ine *51, 136, 137, 138, 139*
Inei Raisan *306, 332*
Intangible Cultural Heritage *17*
Inuyama *59*
irori *283, 302*
ishibadate *263, 321, 322*
Ishibekoji *131, 190, 218, 387, 394*
Ishigaki Island *187*
Ishigaki no Sato *166*
Ito, Shinobu *293, 303*
Ivy Square *151*
Iwami Ginzan *190, 227, 397*
Iwate *320*
Iya *21, 22, 23, 24, 383*
Izu Matsuzaki *189*
Izu Peninsula *212*
Izu stone *285, 286, 309, 310, 311*
Izumifumoto *191, 237, 399*
Izushi *190, 223, 395*

J

Japan Folk Crafts Museum *188, 198*
Japan Heritage site *55*
Japan red *154*
jindai keyaki *283, 284, 295, 296, 297, 310, 311*
Jizo *102, 103, 326*

JMRA *9, 16, 243, 246, 248, 332*
Joetsu *111, 112, 248, 249, 258, 283, 290, 295, 342, 400*

K

Kagoshima *236, 237, 399, 400*
kagura *30, 31*
Kagurazaka *188*
kaiseki *214, 232*
Kaitaku no Mura *50, 58, 59*
Kaiyomaru *54, 55*
Kajikawa's Barbershop *226, 396*
Kakehata, Akimitsu *282*
Kakujoro *189, 213*
Kakunodate *50, 61, 62, 63, 383*
Kamakura *78, 93, 204, 233*
Kameoka *20, 23, 24, 25, 383*
Kameyama, Mie *124, 127, 386*
Kamimachi district *174*
Kamishichiken *190, 221*
Kanagawa *76, 79, 200, 243, 244, 384, 391*
Kanaya *26*
Kanazawa *188, 203, 391*
Kanto *73, 320*
Kappo *197*
Karuizawa *96, 384*
Kasashima *191, 231, 398*
Kasenan Seni Onsen Iwan-oyu *189, 209, 392*
Kashihara *144, 147, 387*
Katakurakan *191, 235, 399*
Kataoka Residence, the *224*

Katori *72, 74, 75, 384*
Katori Kaido *74*
Katsunuma *111, 112, 114, 115, 272, 295, 326, 385, 386*
Katsunuma Winery *111, 385*
Katsura Rikyu *322*
Katsushika Hokusai *206*
Kawaga *231*
Kawagoe *188, 196, 390*
Kawane Onsen *26*
Kawasemi Cottage *26, 29, 30, 31*
kayabuki *133, 201*
Kazui, Masataka *249, 346*
Kazui Family House *251, 378*
Keio era *100*
Kerr, Alex *19, 20, 21*
keyaki *256, 263, 264, 282, 283, 284, 295, 296, 297, 305, 310, 311, 316, 328, 329, 330, 331, 332*
Kiotoshi *268, 269*
Kiragawa *51, 172, 173, 174, 175, 388*
Kiso *104, 107, 207, 208, 385, 392*
Kitakata *188, 195, 390*
Kitamaebune *83*
Kitano Tenmangu Shrine *221*
Kitayama-style *134*
Kitsuki *51, 176, 178, 389*
Kitsuki Castle *178*
Kiyomizu-dera *130, 131*
Kobayashi, Hideki *282*
Koboriya *74*

kobudo *23*
Kochi *172, 174, 175, 233, 388, 398*
Koedo *196*
Kofu *111, 115, 244, 253, 314*
Kofukuan *324*
Korogaki *292*
Koryuen Orchards *112, 385*
Koshinzuka *106, 107, 189, 208, 392*
Koshu *109, 110, 111, 112, 113, 114, 115, 266, 270, 271, 342, 343, 385, 386*
Koshu Valley *109, 110, 111*
koto *26, 242, 243*
Kumagawajuku *188*
Kumezo *329*
Kunisaki Peninsula *176*
kura *148, 195, 211, 282, 283, 330*
Kurakukan Kurajuku *174, 388*
Kuramubon Winery *112, 385*
Kurashiki *51, 148, 150, 151, 387*
Kurayoshi *190, 226, 396*
Kurosawa, Akira *95*
Kuroyu Onsen Inn *188, 193*
Kusakabe Folk Museum *122, 123*
Kusama, Yayoi *103*
Kusunoki, Homare *287, 312, 313, 321, 323, 332, 338, 343, 351, 380*
Kuta *134*
Kyoho *112, 272*

Kyomachidori *82*
Kyoto *8, 20, 23, 24, 25, 61, 62, 78, 81, 82, 104, 121, 124, 128, 129, 130, 131, 132, 133, 134, 136, 137, 139, 204, 207, 217, 218, 219, 220, 221, 248, 277, 322, 383, 386, 387, 394, 395*
Kyoto Project *23*
Kyushu *21, 176, 178, 233*

L

Lake Suwa *268*
lattice doors *329*
LED *332*
Living in Japan *20*
loft *29, 253, 279, 290, 312, 313, 321*
Lost Japan *20*

M

Machida *200, 324, 391*
machiya *24, 131, 218, 341*
Machiya Museum, The *171*
Maezawa hamlet *194*
Magome *106*
Maine *26, 27*
Maison Ancienne *113, 115*
Makigaoka *246, 247, 248, 272, 277, 279, 342, 400*
Makioka *111, 112, 115, 258, 385, 386*
Marufuji Winery *109, 114, 385*

古民家 ◆ *Kominka*

Marumo 100, 101, 103
Maruyama Park 131
Maruyama Taro 103
Matsudai Bengs House 50, 87, 384
Matsue 190, 227, 397
Matsumoto 50, 62, 100, 102, 103, 384
Matsumoto Castle 100
Matsumoto Folkcraft Museum 102, 103
Matsushiroya 106
Matsuzaki 189, 212, 393
Meiji 13, 29, 55, 57, 59, 62, 71, 74, 78, 87, 95, 96, 104, 111, 112, 114, 129, 143, 154, 162, 166, 169, 171, 174, 176, 182, 192, 195, 200, 211, 214, 218, 231, 233, 234, 249, 252, 324, 350
Meiji Restoration 55, 78, 162
Metoba River 100
Mie 124, 127, 386
Mikawa Bay 213, 214
Mikuni 277
Minami Ichijo 58
Minamigaoka Art Museum 50, 384
Mingei 103, 198
Minka Bank 248
Mino 189, 211, 393
Misasa Onsen 190, 226
Mitoku River 226
Miya River 123
Miyama 51, 132, 133, 134, 135, 248, 277

Miyamasou 135
Miyazaki Woodworking 307, 308, 329
Mizuhiki hamlet 194
Mo-an 190, 220
Mori samurai clan 162
Morino Medicinal Herb Garden 224
mortise 326
Mt. Fuji 109, 110, 111, 206, 245, 253, 259, 260, 263, 271, 279, 295, 300, 309, 314, 349
Mt. Hachibuse 202
Mugeiso 189, 208, 392
Murakami House 118
Muromachi 65, 178, 204
Muromachi period 65, 178
Muroto 172, 173, 175, 388
Museum Meiji-Mura 59

N

Nagahama 277
Nagano 92, 94, 95, 96, 99, 100, 102, 104, 107, 205, 206, 207, 208, 209, 235, 268, 384, 385, 392, 399
Nagara River 211
Nakamachi 100, 102, 103, 127, 207, 386
Nakamura Family Merchant House 53, 55
Nakasendo 104, 106, 207
Nakasone, Yasuhiro 199
Nantan 132, 133, 134, 387
Nara 15, 17, 121, 126, 144, 147, 224

Narai 106
Naraijuku 189, 207, 392
National Important Cultural Properties 123
Nawatedori 100
neko-ishi 263, 264
NHK (Japan Broadcasting Corporation) 91
Nihon University 88
Niigata 80, 81, 83, 84, 85, 86, 87, 89, 91, 111, 112, 114, 182, 201, 248, 249, 277, 282, 283, 342, 343, 350, 384, 391, 400
Nineizaka 129
Nippon Suisan 26
Nishioka, Tsunekazu 15
Nishiyama Bekkan 191, 230, 397
Nobesawa Ginzan silver mine 65
Noda, Kogo 208
noh 23, 81, 82
Northern Japan Alps 100
Notoya Ryokan 66, 67
Nozawa, Masao 246, 257, 260, 262, 264, 278, 279, 283, 284, 288, 296, 297, 298, 303, 308, 318, 322, 338, 340, 343, 346, 349
Nozawa Jyuken Co., Ltd. 257, 340
Numazu 27, 189, 211, 393
Numazu Club 189, 211, 393
Nyuto Onsen 193

Index 407

O

Obama *189, 204, 391*
Obama Nishikumi *189, 204*
Obanazawa *64, 66, 383*
Obuse *189, 206, 392*
Ochiai Village *21*
Ogi no le *201, 391*
Oginoshima Village *188, 201, 391*
Ohana *191, 234, 398*
Ohara Museum *151*
Ohashi Ryokan *226*
Oigawa Railway *26, 31*
oinari-san *29*
Oita *176, 179, 180, 182, 183, 235, 236, 389, 399*
Okayama *148, 151, 152, 155, 228, 387, 397*
Okinawa *36, 184, 185, 187, 389*
Omihachiman *189, 215, 394*
Omori Iwami Ginzan *190*
Omura Residence *171*
Onbashira Festival *268*
Ono River *74*
Onomichi *191, 229, 230, 397*
Ontake *277*
Oomoto seminary *23*
Osaka *83, 147, 150, 221, 395*
Oshin *67*
Oshino Village *189, 205*
Ota, Hiroshi *337*
Otaru Canal *188, 192*
Otowa Waterfall *130, 131*
Ouchijuku *50, 68, 69, 70, 71, 383*

Ouda *190, 224, 396*
Oxford University *20*
Ozu, Yasujiro *208, 229*

P

Paris *88, 171*
Paulownia *260*
plastering *17, 293, 294, 303*
post town *69, 71, 93, 106, 163, 204, 207*
public bathhouse *29*

Q

Quartz Black *302, 309, 340*

R

ranma *325, 326*
Reagan, Ronald *199*
residence of the Aoyagi samurai family, the *61*
Rinshunkaku *77, 78*
ronin *95*
ryokan *67, 87, 131, 135, 156, 157, 159, 181, 183, 197, 207, 209, 213, 232, 389, 396*
Ryotsu Ogawa *85, 384*
Ryujin Onsen Kamigoten *190, 225, 396*
Ryukyu *185*

S

Sado Island *50, 81, 83, 84, 85, 95*

Sagatoriimoto *190, 218, 394*
Sakamoto *189*
sake *29, 58, 74, 83, 115, 123, 195, 208, 295, 301, 310, 386*
samurai district *63*
Sangoso *50, 96, 99, 384*
Sankakuya *81, 83*
Sankeien Garden *50, 76, 77, 79, 384*
Sankyoson *188, 202, 277, 391*
Sanneizaka *51, 128, 129, 130, 131*
Sannenzaka *129*
Sansou Murata *51, 180, 181, 183, 389*
Sapporo *56, 58, 59*
Sasama *26, 27, 30, 31, 32*
Sasanamiichi *163*
Sasayama Castle *141*
Sassa Koka *197*
Sato Budo *112*
Satoe Onsen *232*
Sawara *50, 72, 73, 74, 75*
Sawara Grand Festival *73, 75*
scaffolding *294, 300, 301*
Sea of Japan *24, 53, 81, 162, 204*
Sekijuku *50, 124, 126, 127, 386*
Sekikawa Family Villa *55*
Sekishu clay tiles *153, 155*
Sekitei *51, 156, 157, 158, 159, 388*
Sengoku period *336*
Seto Inland Sea *228, 231, 232*

Shangri-La 266
Shiga 215, 216, 248, 277, 394
shiguchi 264
Shikoku 165, 169, 173
Shima no Ie 201, 391
Shimayado Mari 191, 232, 398
Shimizu 27
Shimogo 68, 70, 383
Shimomachi district 174
Shinbashi 190, 217, 245, 394
Shin-Kiba 282
Shinto 58, 126, 154
Shiono, Masami 295, 296, 297
Shiono Lumber Co., Ltd. 295
Shirakawago 50, 78, 116, 118, 123, 396
Shirasu, Jiro 200
Shirasu, Masako 24, 200
Shiratama 189, 394
Shiwaku Islands 231
Shizuoka 26, 27, 31, 32, 211, 212, 383, 393
Shobundo bookstore 74, 75
Shodoshima 232
shoji 18, 27, 63, 106, 254, 255, 288, 289, 306, 307, 308, 331, 332, 337
Shotoen garden 234
Showa 30, 57, 67, 129, 213, 224, 226, 232
Showa era 30
Shukunegi 81, 83, 85, 384
Sick Building Syndrome 334

Sobamaru 114, 385
Sokakuan 89, 90, 91, 351
solid wood 14, 260, 280, 281, 334, 335
Somaguchi 111, 247, 385, 400
Sonobe 24
Sotodomari 51, 164, 165, 166, 388
stone walls 165, 166, 173, 174, 187, 218, 237
Suwa Taisha 268

T

Tachibana clan 234
Tachibana-tei Ohana Estate 191, 234, 398
Tadataka, Ino 74, 75
Taiman 103
Taisho 57, 66, 112, 129, 143, 226
Takahashi 152, 153, 155, 191, 228, 387, 397
Takahashi, Okayama 152, 155, 387, 397
Takayama Castle 123
Takayanagi 201, 391
Takeda Construction 332
Takeda Shingen 114, 292, 336
Takeda, Toyoki 332
Takegawara Onsen 191, 399
Takei, Hirotake 276
Takei, Osamu 276, 277
Takei Sheet Metal Works 276
Takenaka Carpentry Tools 190
Taketokoro 87, 89, 91

Taketomi 51, 184, 185, 186, 187, 389
Taketomi Island 51, 184, 187, 389
Takigi Noh 81
Tale of Genji, The 218
Tamba Sasayama 51, 140, 141, 143, 387
tamo 332
Tangible Cultural Property 55, 211
Tango Peninsula 137
Tanizaki, Junichiro 306
Tan's Bar 182
Tateiwa Village 188, 194, 389
Tateshina 208, 392
Tatsuno 190, 223, 395
Taut, Bruno 88, 91
Tawaraya 190, 395
tea ceremony 23, 157, 159, 242, 243, 254, 278
tenon 18, 326
thatched houses 21, 87, 133, 134
Thirty-six Views of Mt. Fuji 206
Tochigi 71, 188, 195, 390
Tohoku 24
Tokai Saiseki Kogyo Co., Ltd. 285, 286
Tokaido 26, 124, 127, 216, 221
Tokaido Shinkansen 26
Tokamachi 86, 87, 88, 384
tokonoma 303, 305, 316
Tokugawa 55
Tokyo 8, 20, 26, 74, 77, 91, 104, 110, 124, 192, 196, 198, 199, 200, 207,

Index 409

208, 229, 245, 324, 390, 391
Tokyo Story (1953) 208, 229
Tomachi 62
Tomi 92, 94, 384
Tomonoura 191, 228
Tone River 73, 74
topping-out ceremony 270
Tottori 225, 226, 396
Toutouan 188, 199, 390
Toyama 116, 118, 119, 202, 277, 386, 391
Tsuchiya, Tokumitsu 329
Tsuchiya Joinery Shop 329
tsukimidai 322
Tsumago 50, 104, 106, 107, 385
Tsurunoyu 193

U

Uchiko 51, 168, 169, 170, 171, 387
Uchimachi 62, 63
udatsu 94, 95, 231, 398
Udatsu Wall Historical District 211
Uemura 131, 218, 387
UNESCO 17, 117, 118, 126, 130, 131, 227
United States, the 4, 20, 26, 192, 204
University of North Carolina–Chapel Hill 26
University of Washington 26
Unnojuku 50, 92, 93, 94, 95, 384
Usuki 191, 236, 399

W

Wakasa Bay 204
Wakayama 225, 396
Wakimachi Minamimachi 191, 231, 398
Warring States Period 123, 147, 215
washi paper 211, 307, 308, 337
washlet 310
Watanabe, Hidehiko 285
Watanabe, Mitsuru 302, 310
Watanabe Tile Industry 302
Western architecture 15, 16
Western-style 20, 28, 58, 192, 234
Western-style houses 20, 28
Wolverine, The (2013) 228
World Heritage Sites 17, 117, 126

Y

Yada Tenmangu Shrine 23
Yaeyama 184, 185, 187, 389
Yakushiji 15
Yale University 20
Yamagata 64, 65, 66, 383
Yamaguchi 160, 388
Yamanashi 50, 96, 108, 109, 111, 112, 113, 114, 115, 205, 244, 246, 248, 249, 252, 258, 263, 265, 266, 279, 292, 295, 321, 330, 337, 342, 350, 385, 386, 392, 400
Yamanashi Kominka Club 50, 111, 112, 113, 114, 385
Yanagawa 191, 233, 234, 398
Yanagi, Muneyoshi 198
Yasuzuka 249, 342, 400
Yojinbo (1961) 95
Yokaichi district 171
Yokohama 20, 76, 77, 79, 200, 242, 246, 263, 288, 295, 317, 320, 321, 329, 331, 391
Yokoyama Taikan 78
Yoro Shuzo 115, 386
Yosa 136, 139, 387
Yosabei Guesthouse 85, 384
Yoshijima Residence 123
Yufuin 178, 180, 181, 183, 389
Yunoshimakan 189, 210, 393
Yusuhara 191, 233, 398

Z

zelkova 214, 248, 249, 263, 282, 284, 348, 349
Zenkoji 95

古民家 ♦ *Kominka*

ABOUT THE AUTHOR

Kazuo Hasegawa has lived a life in real estate. He launched his career in the Japanese housing industry as publisher of the widely circulated periodical, *Jutaku Joho,* which listed properties for rent, sale, and investment. A passionate believer in the cultural significance of traditional Japanese old houses and the importance of their preservation, he was instrumental in the founding of the nonprofit Japan Minka Revival Association (JMRA), of which he is a permanent director. A world traveler and photographer, he has contributed articles and images to various books, newspapers, magazines, and exhibitions in his native country. He divides his time between a condominium in Yokohama City and a restored 100-year-old kominka in rural Yamanashi, where he created and runs Gallery Wa as a hub for art and heritage enthusiasts.